AF540987

SP
Pvt. Ltd.

Globalization And Democratic Values

Tamanna Khosla
Assistant Professor
Department of Political Science
Delhi College of Arts and Commerce
New Delhi – 110 023

Rashmi Jain
Director
Centre for the Study of Social Exclusion and Inclusive Policy
University of Rajasthan
Jaipur – 302 004

2019

Studium Press (India) Pvt. Ltd.

Globalization And Democratic Values

ISBN: 978-93-85046-34-6

Published by:

Studium Press (India) Pvt. Ltd.
4735/22, 2nd Floor, Prakash Deep Building
(Near Delhi Medical Association),
Ansari Road, Darya Ganj, New Delhi-110 002
Tel.: + 91-11-43240200-15 (15 lines); Fax: 91-11-43240215
E-mail: pubdir@studiumpress.in

Printed at India

About the Editor(s)

Dr. Tamanna Khosla

Tamanna Khosla has done her MA, M.Phil and PhD from JNU, Delhi on Multi-Culturalism and Feminism. She has done her Bachelors from Lady Shri Ram College. She has worked as Research Associate in many Research Institutes such as JNU, WISCOMP and CSR. Currently she is Assistant Professor in Delhi College of Arts and Commerce in Department of Political Science. She has also been teaching in Department of Political Science, DU at Masters Level.

Dr. Rashmi Jain

Dr Rashmi Jain, Associate Professor, Department of Sociology, University of Rajasthan, Jaipur has her interest in the area of Development Communication, Gender studies, Sociology of Law, leisure studies and European Studies. She has been regularly taking part in conferences and seminars both in the country and abroad and has been active in organizing national and international conferences. She is widely travelled having presented papers in South Africa, Sweden, Spain, Argentina, Germany, Japan,

China and Austria. She is Convener of Working Group on Law and Migration of International Sociological Association. At present she is Vice principal, University maharani College and director, Centre for Jain Studies, UOR, Jaipur. She has four books published to her credit. Her latest book *Global Leisure and the Struggle for a Better World* has been published by Palgrave Macmillan. She has written more than 20 research papers in national and international journals. She is Convener of Research committee on Sociology of Law of Indian Sociological Society. She has Besides being an academician, she has been working for raising voice for destitute women and citizen's issues by collaborating with civil society organizations of Rajasthan. She has been Joint Secretary of Rajasthan University Women's Association for four years. At present she is Convener of Academic Cell of RUWA. She is Founder Secretary of SUMEDHA, an NGO working in the field of education since 1999. Through SUMEDHA, she provides financial assistance to 500 needy poor students for higher education every year. Till now she has helped more than 6000 students in pursuit of higher education.

Preface

The Democracy Manifesto signals that the time has come to open ourselves to the many ways in which the demos, that is, the people, organize themselves around the world to take charge of their own destiny.

When demonstrations against the government start to take place even in such sleepy places as Swaziland, one knows democracy is on progress worldwide. People worldwide are not ready to take non democratic setup. Arab autocrats like Hosni Mubarak and Muammar Gaddafi are criticized for their intention to perpetuate themselves in power through their offspring. But this happens in democracies too where there are dynasts ruling in political parties be it regional or central parties, example being India.

The much more significant question raised in the course of 2011 so far is that of the relationship between globalization and democracy.

Globalization, that is, the steady rise in trans-border flows of goods, services, capital, symbols and cultural products that we have seen over the past three decades or so, has gone hand in hand with an equally steady expansion of democratic ideas around the world. This has led to importing of democracy across globe. This was also witnessed after collapse of communist countries which tried venturing towards democracy. The notion that people ought to rule themselves and through their representatives - and not through some self-appointed masters - has percolated in most of the worlds nation states whether Islamic or communist. Yet, while the central idea of democracy as self-rule, in its broad contours, is the same everywhere, the specific manifestations of it will vary from region to region and from country to country.

Democracy is spreading and it will be with us to stay. That is the good news.

Globalization, by spreading the idea of democracy, has helped to liberate people from dictatorial means of governance. But globalization also embodies the danger that a 'one-size fits all' model of democracy be imposed from abroad and from above. This is a problem as many Islamic countries believe in a different kind of system based on Shariat. So reconciling democracy with Shariat is difficult if not impossible fact.

We currently do live in the information society. The information society, in turn, is based on networks, a new, less hierarchical way of structuring organizations, and one in which the new currency of the realm is knowledge and the ability to handle it. But also the difficulty which democracies face in a negative manner is increase in surveillance on the citizenry and international realm. Be it communist China or democratic US and India. Due to increase in crime of all kinds this sort of surveillance though dangerous has also become necessary.

This has also meant an upsurge of efforts to categorize, classify and rank countries around the world according to a variety of 'democracy indexes', which purport to tell us how democratic any given country is.. Funds are disbursed, loans are approved or rejected and countries are suspended from international organizations as a result of these rankings.

Throughout the Global South we are witnessing the rise of newly emerging powers, that will set the tone for much of the twenty-first century. The fastest-growing and most dynamic economies today are not in the North, but in the South. Not all of them are democracies. But India is the largest democracy in the world. It is living proof that many of the standard verities about the so-called 'prerequisites for democracy' developed in the political science literature in the fifties and sixties, and largely inspired by the history of North Atlantic countries, have limited application elsewhere. Similarly we need to see after the collapse of Soviet Union how much of democracy which is liberal in nature has developed in Russia. Also the need for development of democracy in African states like Morocco can be seen now. The time has come to deparochialize our notion of democracy, to cease to believe that it has exclusively western roots and forms, and to open ourselves to the many ways in which the *demos*, that is, the people, organize themselves around the world to take charge of their own destiny. Democracy thus needs to be redefined as a new world order is there to develop.

Editors

Table of Contents

1

Is Democracy A Universal Concept?[1]

Tamanna Khosla[1]*

ABSTRACT

Democracy is considered to be the best form of government these days but even in democratic countries the very thought behind democracy is not universally followed. Most of the countries in the world have adopted it. Explore the need to understand whether democracy is morally desirable in all polities? Can democracy provide the answer or any other form of governance practiced in world can provide the rejoinder. Can democracy be considered a universal conception of governance or can countries like in middle east, Africa, China and Russia provide the lead to have their own kind of democracy?

***Key words*:** Democracy, Liberty, Reasonableness, Overlapping consensus.

[1] Department of Political Science, Delhi College of Arts and Commerce, Delhi University

**Corresponding E-mail*: tamannakhosla@gmail.com

[1]Republished from intellectual resonance.

I

The researchers in the article explore the need to understand whether democracy is morally desirable in all polities? Can democracy provide the answer or any other form of governance practiced in world can provide the rejoinder. Can democracy be considered a universal conception of governance or can countries like in middle east, Africa, china and Russia provide the lead to have their own kind of democracy?

II

Democracy is considered to be the best form of government these days but even in democratic countries the very thought behind democracy is not universally followed. Most of the countries in the world have adopted it. But before we understand this concept, we need to understand what is democracy? Here, first the researchers look at some of the basic principles on which a democracy is based.

1. LIBERTY

Some argue that the basic principles of democracy are founded in the idea that each individual has a right to liberty. Democracy, it is said, extends the idea that each ought to be master of his or her life to the domain of collective decision making. First, each person's life is deeply affected by the larger social, legal and cultural environment in which he or she lives. Second, only when each person has an equal voice and vote in the process of collective decision-making will each have control over this larger environment. Thinkers such as Carol Gould (1988, pp. 45–85) conclude that only when some kind of democracy is implemented, will individuals have a chance at self-government.

2. DEMOCRACY AS PRINCIPLE OF REASONABLENESS AND RECIPROCITY

The basic principle seems to be the principle of reasonableness according to which reasonable persons will only offer principles for the regulation of their society that other reasonable persons can reasonably accept. The notion of the reasonable is meant to be fairly weak on this account. One can reasonably reject a doctrine to the extent that it is incompatible with one's own doctrine as long as one's doctrine does not imply imposition on others and it is a doctrine that has survived sustained critical reflection. So this principle is a kind of principle of reciprocity.

3. DEMOCRACY AS OVERLAPPING CONSENSUS

When individuals offer proposals for the regulation of their society, they ought not to appeal to the whole truth as they see it but only to that part of the whole truth that others can reasonably accept. To put the matter in the way Rawls puts it: political society must be regulated by principles on which there is an overlapping consensus (Rawls, 1996; Lecture IV). This is meant to obviate the need for a complete consensus on the principles that regulate society. Moreover, it is hard to see how this approach avoids the need for a complete consensus, which is highly unlikely to occur in any even moderately diverse society.

4. DEMOCRACY AS COMPROMISE AMONG CONFLICTING CLAIMS

On one version, defended by Peter Singer (1973, pp. 30 – 41), when people insist on different ways of arranging matters properly, each person in a sense claims a right to be dictator over their shared lives. But these claims to dictatorship cannot all hold up, the argument goes. Democracy embodies a kind of peaceful and fair compromise among these conflicting claims to rule. Each compromises equally on what he claims as long as the others do, resulting in each having an equal say over decision making. In effect, democratic decision making respects each person's point of view on matters of common concern by giving each an equal say about what to do in cases of disagreement (Singer, 1973; Waldron, 1999; Chap. 5).

After looking at what constitutes democracy, I would look at how democracy has evolved over the centuries and its stages.

III STAGES OF DEMOCRACY

3.1. Democracy as Blindness to Difference

Democracy and liberalism in some way linked principles. Democracy can't exist without liberalism and liberalism can't exist without liberalism. Liberal democratic theory in its first stage was based on certain core principles. First, such assumptions is that democratic liberal theory is individualistic in asserting or assuming the moral primacy of the person against the claims of any social collectivity. Second that it is egalitarianism or based on equality, because, it confers on all such individuals the same moral status and denies the relevance to legal or political order of difference in moral worth among human beings. Third it is universalist because it affirms the moral unity of the human species and accords a secondary importance to specific historical association and cultural forms. (Kukathas, 1992; 108).

Historically these very characteristics formed the bedrock of Renaissance, reformation, French revolution and American civil war (some of the most eloquent articulation of democratic aspiration) which questioned social prejudice wherein class and race were used to justify exclusion and discrimination in the public and political domain (Mahajan, 1998; 2). Similar movement post independence was launched by Gandhi and Dr B.R. Ambedkar against caste oppression in India. Slowly and gradually women movement added its voice and demanded right in democracy to vote. They further demanded right to freedom from oppression, right to work outside and against drudgery of work within the family. Dissenting religious groups for instance Catholics and Jews in England and Protestants in France also employed the principle of equality to question their exclusion from public life (Mahajan, 1998; 2).

As far as theorizing about democracy was concerned, the notion of natural equality was supplemented by the idea that all persons as members of human species possess equal dignity and deserve the same respect and consideration. This perception has been derived from writings of Immanuel Kant whose reference to universal humanity bolstered the notion of equality, freedom and gave a new edge to the struggle of marginalized population. He spoke about individualism by highlighting that Enlightenment is about thinking for oneself rather than letting others think for you. In this essay, Kant also expresses the Enlightenment faith in the inevitability of progress. The most important belief about things in themselves that Kant thinks only practical philosophy can justify concerns human freedom. Freedom is important because, on Kant's view, moral appraisal presupposes that we are free in the sense that we have the ability to do otherwise.

Thinkers like Rawls advocated Rawls that civil and political rights and primary social goods such such as education and employment should not be distributed on the basis of ascriptive character that are arbitrary from moral point of view. Rights and benefits, privileges and power, should be distributed in a manner that is blind to social differences. At minimum, justice requires a regime of fair equality of opportunity, ungirded by a system of equal rights and liberty for all citizens.

To Rawls since the difference among parties are unknown to them and everyone is equally rational and similarly situated, therefore we can view the original position from the standpoint of one persons selected at random. Thus Rawls theory differences at the outset from his thought.

Thus while upholding the rule of law may require intervention in the affairs of individuals and groups, but liberal politics is not concerned with these affairs in themselves. Indeed it is indifference to particular human affairs or to particular pursuits of individuals and groups. Liberalism might well be described as the 'politics of indifference (Kukathas, 1998).

Thus logical conclusion of these principles seem to be color blind constitution, the removal of all legislation, the removal of all legislations differentiating people in terms of their race or ethnicity (except for temporary measures like affirmative action), extending the meaning of equality through supreme court cases, which are believed necessary to reach towards such a color blind society.

3.2. Democracy Defined as Respect to Otherness

However once civil and political rights were granted to all persons and class, color and gender were no longer the basis of excluding people from the political domain, thinking about differences underwent considerable change. Thus far the principle of equality had offered a criterion of inclusion and disenfranchised population had used it to demand an equal voice in political process. But once this particular goal had been fulfilled, social differences began to resurface again and assert themselves without the accompanying fear of legitimizing discrimination (Mahajan, p. 7).

Increasingly in this changed environment attention was given on arguments by feminist, cultural and racial difference theorists who stressed on the notion of democracy as need to embrace difference. Thus, democracy needs to incorporate otherness. This provided a critique of the liberal notion of equality. In fact the ideologues of the new ideal were critical of formal equality on the ground that it obliterated differences but also brought forth the aspect of distinct irreducible identities across color, creed, religion and gender. By categorizing the members of state as citizens the democratic polity ignored the difference between them.

Further liberal democracy emphasis on distinction between public and private sphere was critiqued by feminists and cultural/ racial rights theorists. According to them, this led to establishment of secular public sphere where individual which was neutral and indifferent to differences in nature; the private sphere was one where multiple differences found place. This democracy during this phase saw view point of minorities and women being relegated to private sphere (while public sphere was where the dominant western Anglo Saxon norms operated as neutral in nature). According to them aim of equality or anti discrimination legislation is the production of sameness, ignoring differences in women and minority perspective.

Therefore when notion of difference is invoked by these groups what is being asked to recognize is the unique identity of this individual or group, their distinctness from others. The idea is that it is precisely this distinctness that has been ignored, glossed over, assimilated to a dominant or majority identity. And this assimilation is the cardinal sin against the ideal of authenticity (Taylor, 1994; p. 82).

It was in keeping with the thought the emphasis shifted from pursuit of illusionary goal of equality towards affirmation of irreducible differences of erstwhile marginalized groups. Such a notion has been powerfully presented within certain feminist, racial and cultural difference literature.

Democracy encouraged feminist to reclaim the feminine and women liberation lay in affirmation of their irreducible differences rather than in pursuit of illusionary goal of equality. Few of the most sophisticated works on the notion of difference have been result of writings of French feminists. Simone de Beauvoir can be considered a figure to whom all feminists owe some debt for introducing the question of a differently sexed body.

French psychoanalyst have been highly skeptical of attribution of a negative value to women's relation to language (that is they talk of how womens relation to language, where binaries are constructed - one term example man/mind/reason is given a positive value through being positioned as primary in relation to an opposite term which is negatively coded-women/body/passion) and of sexism implicit of the elevation of phallus to the place of transcendental signifier. Such a system according to Helene Cixous is referred as phallocentric. Her writing seeks to disrupt this symbolic order. In line with this critique, Cixous in her work aims a blow at phallogocentric culture where it hurts the most and attacks it for marking women as the other, as different, as negativity (Cixous, 1976). She questions the repression of feminine in culture and provocatively questions masculine language. Luce Irigaray takes as her point of departure an indictment of psychoanalysis for its almost total disregard of the female subject and therefore she speaks of relationship of women to women, by opening a space in which women "speak female and speak to each other without the interference of men (Irigaray, 1980).

Democratic system also encouraged lot of feminists to express opinion on difference between men and women. Apart from French feminists, radical feminists too describe how oppression takes place in democracy which is largely patriarchal in nature.

3.3. Democracy as Diversity

Democracy as diversity was unleashed with a movement for multiculturalism in the seventies. It spread first in Canada and Australia to be subsequently followed in US, UK, Germany and elsewhere. Such a democracy fights for the rights of women and minorities in a new way by subverting the truth claims of all who exclude them. Such a democracy feels that fundamental concern is not economics but esteem, not income but identity. Therefore there is shift from sixties emphasis of political economy to identity politics. The focus of this kind of democracy is on the welfare of people or cultural groupings, which are seen as the source of the socially constructed identities of individuals. Therefore as against previous democracies stress on politics of indifference, the new democracy advocated a politics of difference, endorsing diversity not only as a fact but also as a value, albeit as most would stress cultural diversity. Difference is not merely to be understood as discrimination or as otherness in an absolute sense with no dialogue possible, but more so as representing diverse opinions and voices of marginalized groups-which were now not only race, religion, gender but also cultural difference between communities, their way of life, system or moral values, modes of dress and address which were to be weighed positively.

In this phase of democracy, theorists advocate politics of difference as against a politics of equal dignity. The politics of difference as Taylor explains it, does not merely allow traditions a run for their money, it is committed to their flourishing. Whereas politics of equal dignity focuses on what is same in all, the politics of difference asks us to recognize and even foster particularity as the first principle. Whereas the politics of universal dignity fought for forms of non discrimination that were quite blind to the ways in which citizens differ, the politics of difference often redefines non discrimination as requiring that we make those distinctions the basis of differential treatment. No culture is wholly worthless, that it deserves atleast some respect because of what it means to its members and the creative energy it display, that no culture is perfect and has a right to impose itself on others and the culture are best changed from within.(Parekh, 1999; 15).

Thus today, democrats reflect upon the special but diverse needs of minorities, immigrants and indigenous people. Not only opportunity for them to survive but also stress is on to provide minorities, Immigrants and indigenous people. Group differentiated minority rights include people both as citizens and as members of specific community. In fact Chantal Mouffe through her notion of radical democratic citizenship challenges the liberal public/private distinction to bring out that there can be as many forms of citizenship as there can be interpretation of these principles (Mouffe, 1998).

Further democrats emphasize on irreducible particularity and complex diversity characterizing the lives of non western world.

For example several feminists like Chandra Talpade Mohanty show how category of third world women is appropriated by western feminists as ultimate proof of patriarchy and female bondage (Mohanty, 1984) To Gayatri Spivak, it is ludicrous to talk of specificity of female body. It follows that for a women that heterogeneity most importantly include the experience of her body, an experience which has been subject to the most rigorous male censorship down the ages and finds a particularly shocking but exemplary form in the practice of clitoredectomy (Spivak, 1987). Further Sylvia Wal by would point the fact that there are different sites of oppression and potentially different sites of struggle. Thus democrats would point out that sites of oppression of colored people may be different from those of white people.

Therefore as Anne Phillips would point out that questions of democracy and difference are the one's that lie at the heart of contemporary dilemma in democracy (Phillips, 1993).

IV DIFFERENT DEMOCRACIES IN DIFFERENT CONTEXTS

No where democracy is functioning in a universal fashion. Each country has its own version of democracy. In this article I look at three regions, that is China, the Muslim countries, Russia and their take on democracy. Each region has developed its own version of democracy. For example in China, Western constitutional democracy", is feared because it would put the Communist Party under the rule of law, not above it. Other threats cited in the memo were promoting "universal values" of human rights, Western-inspired ideas of news-media independence and civic participation, ardently pro-market "neo-liberalism" and "nihilist" criticisms of the party's past. (New York Times) No one has expected China to become a democracy overnight or adopt a Western model. But in recent years there have been some tentative moves toward political liberalization. In 2011-12, for instance, villagers of Wukan in southeast China organized protests against land grabs and ended up forcing elections and driving out local leaders. Many hoped that Mr. Xi, who took office last year, would push even wider political reforms. His goal is to expand market-driven reforms; this can happen only if he and other leaders relax state control and involve more Chinese and foreign investors in the economy.

But China is deep into an economic transformation that depends on integration with the rest of the world. And the future success of China's economy depends on a steadily more open society of the sort that Chinese liberals and moderates are pushing for. Yet when it comes to the subject of representative democracy in China, For example, most westerners will be surprised to learn that China already holds more elections than any other nation in the world. Under the Organic Law of the Village Committees, all of China's approximately 1 million villages – home to some 600 million voters – hold elections every three years for local village committees. In September 2010, President Hu gave a speech in Hong Kong in which he called for new thinking about Chinese democracy. (Guardian, 2011) Said Hu "There is a need to ... hold democratic elections according to the law; have democratic decision-making, democratic management, as well as democratic supervision; safeguard people's right to know, to participate, to express and to supervise". Wen said that without reforms of the political system, gains from reforms of the economic system would go down the drain. Political reform is necessary, said Wen, to sustain the nation's breakneck economic growth, including opportunities for citizens to criticise and monitor the government.

Most sinologists believe that if Chinese democracy continues to develop, it is unlikely to be an exact copy of the western model. Many are intrigued by the vision promoted by Confucian-inspired intellectuals like Jiang Qing, who have put forward an innovative proposal for a tricameral legislature. Legislators in one chamber would be selected based on merit and competency, and in the others based on elections of some kind. One elected chamber may be reserved only for Communist party members, the other for representatives elected by everyday Chinese. Such a tricameral legislature, its proponents believe, would better ensure that political decisions are made by more educated and enlightened representatives, instead of the rank populism of western - style elected factions.

It's intriguing to contemplate China evolving into some sort of innovative democratic experiment, combining tricameralism with all the high-tech features of deliberative democracy methods to mold a new type of political accountability, as well as separation of powers. Daniel Bell, a Canadian-born professor of political theory at Tsinghua University in Beijing, says China may be groping toward "a political model that works better than western-style democracy". The debate over its form and definition as well as application was one of the major ideological battlegrounds in Chinese politics for well over a century. It is still a contentious subject. Andrew Nathan wrote in his 1985 study that "the Chinese have aspired to democracy as they understand it for a hundred years, have claimed to have it for seventy, and for the last thirty five years have lived in one of the most participatory societies in history." In December 2008, more than 350 intellectual and cultural leaders, including Liu Xiaobo, issued Charter 08. The Charter said China remains the only large world power to still retain an authoritarian system that so infringes on human rights, and "This situation must change! Political democratic reforms cannot be delayed any longer!

Further Most Muslims Want Democracy, Personal Freedoms, and Islam in Political Life But few Believe in U.S. Backed Democracy. More than a year after the first stirrings of the Arab Spring, there continues to be a strong desire for democracy in Arab and other predominantly Muslim nations. Solid majorities in Lebanon, Turkey, Egypt, Tunisia and Jordan believe democracy is the best form of government, as do a plurality of Pakistanis.

Indeed, these publics do not just support the general notion of democracy – they also embrace specific features of a democratic system, such as competitive elections and free speech. Enthusiasm for democracy tends to be generally less intense in Jordan and in Pakistan. It is consistently strong in Lebanon and Turkey. While democratic rights and institutions are popular, they are clearly not the only priorities in the six Muslim majority nations surveyed. In particular, the economy is a top concern. And if they had to choose, most Jordanians, Tunisians and Pakistanis would rather have a strong economy than a good democracy. Turks and Lebanese, on the other hand, would prefer democracy. Egyptians are divided.

One of the most prominent Islamic feminist Irshad Manji in her work establishes for the need of reform in Islam. Irshad had founded project Ijtihad, an initiative to renew Islams own tradition of critical thinking, debate and dissent. Project Ijtihad is helping to build the world's most inclusive network of reform-minded muslims and non muslim allies. Her basic argument is that the Koran is a complex, contradictory, human book. Its prescriptions are many and conflicting. "Only group of muslims with the actual freedom to question, criticize and debate has decided to retreat into victim logy and appeasement. "She wants to embrace her faith by understanding it fully, by realizing its vision of human equality, by looking at the ancient Islamic tradition of Ijtihad,: questioning, asking, and thinking". Even Egyptian feminist Nawal el Saadawi writes that" we have to compare the Koran to other holy books before we judge Islam. A fair comparison will help us to discover that the Koran or fundamental teachings of Islam are relatively progressive in relation to democracy and Islam. Takhayur is another concept which aims at eclectic choice from different schools of Islamic tought. Thus the one which is more favorable for rights of men and women need to be adopted.

"As far as Russia is concerned the country seems to have laws that limit the rights and freedoms of people, attack on the news media and organizations of civil society. At the same time, though, Russians were very negative about political exports from the United States — just 26 percent said they liked American ideas about democracy. While many Russians disagree with the Kremlin about who is behind the recent protests in Moscow and other cities, most agree that Russia's political future should be its own. Instead, Russian leaders have found it is far easier and more expedient to talk about already being a democracy while running a state that — beneath the rhetoric — remains as authoritarian as ever. The talk helps to insulate Moscow from the harsh criticism that is leveled upon states that reject democratic values. And it helps to disarm critics by holding out the possibility that tomorrow — if not today — the promises of democracy may yet become reality. Important institutions of democracy, such as fair and free elections, transparency of state structures and freedom of speech have been curbed rather than fostered since Putin's ascended to power. People confirm the need for Russia to find an alternative to the form of Western Liberal democracy. Russia was moving in the right direction in the 1990s, but with the arrival of Putin, democratic reform was reversed and an authoritarian or semi - authoritarian state was established. The second narrative argues that the failure of democracy in Russia is due to the conservative values of the Russian population and its underdeveloped political culture. "Society awakened," in the democratic protests that erupted after the rigged parliamentary elections of December 2011. But the Putin regime responded "by manipulation, the purpose of which was self-preservation at any price.

V CONCLUSION

Democracy as Intermingling of Indigenous Culture with External Influence

Democracy worldwide today is largely a result of intermingling of indigenous culture with external influence. Or would it be apt to say that democracy has been accepted differently in different civilization. In an era of pervasive migration, media globalization and transnational information flow, democracy as a movement has gained momentum even though roots and meanings of each of these movements may be differ from nation to nation. While as post colonialist would say that colonize is inevitably shaped by the experience of colonization, similarly democracy gets shaped by the spirit of globalization. As a result a conceptions of distinct, singular, internal, homogeneous movement gives way to a model of hybridity, of borrowing and lending across porous cultural boundaries on the very notion of democratic nation. The concept of hybridity as Robert Young would note, makes difference into samemess and sameness into difference, but in a way that makes the same no longer same, different no longer different, thereby engendering difference and sameness in an apparently impossible simultaneity. This means that democractic nations might be different in some sense but also similar in some. While differences need to be respected, similarities between democratic polities need to be fostered. As far as sameness is concerned some key elements irrespective of cultural milieu needs to be accepted. Thus metaphors of hybridity and the like not only recognize differences within the subject, fracturing and complicating holistic notion of identity that is democracy but also address connection between subject by recognizing the affiliation, crosspollination, echoes and repetitions. Rather than demarcate certain concepts (modernity, equality, humanism) as intrinsically western and thus forever tied to enforcement of an imperialist agenda, recent theorists are attentive to diverse appropriation and re articulation of such vocabulary across various global site. Each civilization has evolved its own kind of democratic concepts.

The complex intermingling of indigenous tradition and external influence are such that discourses once linked to colonizers or the western world may acquire very different meanings when adopted by colonized to challenge their own tradition. Thus recent readings of modernity have pointed to its internal complexities and uneven temporalities, arguing that white women and people of color have not been outside of modernity but have been shaped by and in turn variously have shaped its political, cultural and philosophical meanings.

Therefore the need is to look at various categories, that is ideology, women, race, culture, in term of difference with sameness and sameness with difference, a form of interface with the purity of such categories, therefore being more open to multiple and mutable concerns than does the appeal to incommensurability and otherness which necessarily leaves the realm of same untouched.

However point needs to be stressed that the new universalism that accommodates cultural, gender and plurality of other sorts in contrast to rainbow epistemology stresses towards communication of knowledge and a politics of global cohabitation rather towards global rainbow democracy.

For example Susan Stanford Friedman has recently made a detailed and compelling case for hybridity and Syncretism as a way of working through certain dilemma s and deadends in feminist theory. Steven Connor infact points out that appeals to difference and incommensurability within poststructural theory always refers back to norms, values and universalizable assumptions. As against particularism, which is a self defeating logic in order to build a more viable multiculturalism, the need would be as laclau would point for formulating universal as an empty place the universalism is not one. It is not a preexisting something to which individuals accede, but rather the fragile, a shifting and always incomplete achievement of political action; it is not a container of a substantive content but all empty place. As laclau puts it, the dimension of universality reached to equivalence is very different from the universality which results from an underlying essence or an unconditioned apriori principle. Rather than thinking of universal as something that is extra political and that can be used to adjudicate political claims. We should think it as a product of political practice. The authentic universal would really be inclusive of all people of race, class, gender, sexuality, ethnicity, nationality, ideology. Need would be to look into the imbrications of the universal and particular, the matter being not choosing one over the other but articulating in a scrupulously political sense, the relation between the two, and how each is rendered impure by irreducible presence of others.

REFERENCES

Cohen, J. (2002). "*Procedure and Substance in Deliberative Democracy*". *In: Philosophy and Democracy*. Christiano, T. (*ed.*), Oxford: Oxford University Press.

Cixous, Helena (1976). "*The Laugh of Medusa*". *Signs, Journal of Women and Culture,* 4.

Chandran Kukathas (1992). "*Are There Any Cultural Rights*", *Political Theory,* 20(1).

Gould, C. (1988). *Rethinking Democracy: Freedom and Social Cooperation in Politics, Economics and Society*, New York: Cambridge University Press.

Irigaray, Luce (1980). "*When our Lips Speak together*". *In*: *Language, Sexuality and Subversion.* Foss, P. and Morris, M. (*ed.*), Darlington, NSW. Feral Public.

——————————— (1998). *Liberalism and Multiculturalism – The Politics of Indifference, Political Theory*, 26(1).

Mahajan Gurpreet (1998). *Democracy, Difference and Social Justice*, Oxford University Press.

Mohanty, Chandra T. (1984). "*Under Western Eyes: Feminist Scholarship and Colonial Discourse*". *Boundary*, 213(1).

Mouffe, Chantal (1993). *The Return of Political*, London: Verso.

Parekh, Bhikhu (1999). *RethinkingMulticulturalism*, Hound Mills: Macmillan Press.

Phillips, Anne (1993). *Democracy and Difference*, Cambridge: Polity press.

Rawls, J. (1996). *Political Liberalism*, New York: Columbia University Press, revised edition.

Singer, P. (1973). *Democracy and Disobedience*, Oxford: Oxford University Press.

Spivak, Gayatri (1987). *In Other Worlds*, New York. Metheun.

Taylor, Charles (1994). "*The Politics of Recognition*". *In*: *Multiculturalism: A Critical Reader.* Goldberg, David T. (*ed.*), UK. Basil Blackwell.

Waldron, J. (1999). *Law and Disagreement*, Oxford: Oxford University Press.

2

An Inclusive Democracy

PETER EMERSON[1]*

ABSTRACT

Democracy is often interpreted to mean majority rule. Accordingly, many decisions in parliaments and / or referendums are taken by a (simple or weighted) majority vote; secondly, governance is often conducted by the party or coalition which commands a majority of the seats in parliament. Majority rule, however, has been (not the but) a cause of violence in many plural societies. Furthermore, majority voting can be inaccurate. A more precise, and therefore more democratic methodology, a preferential points system, is also non-majoritarian. If, then, it were the international democratic norm, there would be no further justification for majority rule. So, with many examples from across the globe, this article first criticises majority voting and its consequence, majority rule. Next, it outlines the more precise Modified Borda Count, MBC. And finally, it describes an inclusive political structure based on appropriate voting procedures in decision-making, elections and in governance.

Key words: Consensus voting, All-party power-sharing, Modified Borda Count, MBC, Matrix vote, Quota Borda System, QBS; Preferential decision-making.

[1] The De Borda Institute, 36 Ballysillan Road, Belfast BT14 7QQ, Northern Ireland

**Corresponding E-mail*: www.deborda.org, pemerson@deborda.org

1. INTRODUCTION

Majority voting has been used by numerous dictators–Napoleon, Mussolini, Hitler, Pinochet, Khomeini and others (Emerson, 2012: 143-50). They choose the question and, except for Pinochet's third referendum, the question is the answer. Some rather more democratic leaders have also tried to dominate politics in this way, and with some notable exceptions, they have often succeeded. The conclusion is stark: majority voting often identifies, not the will of the people, not even the will of the majority, but only the will of he – it's usually a he – who chose the question. Furthermore, majority rule has been a major part of the problem in numerous conflicts – they include Northern Ireland, the Balkans, the Caucasus, Rwanda, South Sudan, Sri Lanka, and not least throughout the Middle East.

Now in a democracy, it is said, elections should be open and transparent. As often as not, however, these are then followed by a process which is at best closed and opaque: the newly elected politicians go upstairs and draw the curtains... and everybody has to wait outside for days, weeks, even months, until the parliamentarians inside have formed a new coalition government. Sometimes, the outcome is not good, for that coalition may well include an extremist party and/or totally exclude an ethno-religious minority.

Accordingly, this article first critiques majority voting from a theoretical standpoint, and then recalls a number of instances in which such binary ballots have been a cause of bitter suffering. Next it describes and analyses a more accurate voting procedure. And finally, it outlines the structure of a more democratic polity.

1.1. A Brief History of Majority

Majority voting was first used in Ancient Greece, albeit only by the male citizenry. But there were no political parties in those days, (Ste Croix, 2005: 198), so people could vote with each other on one day, and against one another the next, without falling into permanently entrenched, mutually antagonistic blocs. At about the same time, binary voting was also used in the former Han Dynasty in China, but only among the ministers in the Imperial Court. Elsewhere, in Africa for example, people relied on a purely verbal process, and if agreement were not reached on one day, the elders would return on the morrow to continue their search for an inclusive solution.

In those old days in Greece, then, majority voting worked fairly well, and only later, in a Roman court of law, did its deficiencies first come to light. So it was that in AD 105, Pliny the Younger devised plurality voting. Next, of course, came the Dark Ages.

In the second millennium, European and then American democracy began to re-emerge, initially only among the barons and boyars of the monarchs' inner circles, but later in people's assemblies and parliaments. Meanwhile, theoreticians started to look at how best collective decisions could be made. Unanimity, of course, was often difficult if not impossible to achieve; so it was concluded that the democratic process was supposed to identify that option which embodied "the greatest good for the greatest number," to quote Jeremy Bentham's phrase.

This use of the superlative implies that the choice should be multi-optional, as befits a pluralist democracy, and various theoreticians experimented with multi-optional and even preferential methodologies. Ramón Llull was the first in 1199, and he spoke of what came to be known as the Borda and Condorcet rules. Nicholas Cusanus followed in 1435, when he suggested that a Borda count, BC, could be used for the election of the Holy Roman Emperor. But the real breakthrough came in France in the 18th Century, when both Jean-Charles de Borda and Le Marquis de Condorcet devised, studied and researched two forms of preferential voting. The politicians, however, both then and now, prefer binary voting.

2. MAJORITARIANISM

There have been a number of instances where this ancient and divisive majority voting has had far-reaching and often terrible consequences.

2.1. Bolshevism

In 1903, at a meeting of the All-Russian Congress of Social Democrats, Vladimir Ilyich Lenin won a vote by 19 to 17, with 3 abstentions (Deutscher, 1982: 71). So he won not a majority but only the larger minority. He nevertheless called himself a Bolshevik – the word means 'member of the majority' (большинство or *bolshinstvo*) – while those of the smaller minority, (меньшинство, *menshinstvo*) became the Mensheviks.

2.2. The Right of Self-determination

In 1920, Ireland opted out of the United Kingdom. So Northern Ireland opted out of Ireland. Similarly, some 70 years later, Georgia opted out of the Soviet Union, so Abhazia opted out of Georgia. Or take the Balkans: Croatia opted out of Yugoslavia, so the Krajina tried to opt out of Croatia. Bosnia was even more complex and, to quote Sarajevo's famous newspaper, *Oslobodjenje*, "all the wars in the former Yugoslavia started with a referendum," (*op. cit.*, 7. 2. 1999). The same now applies to Ukraine and its war of 2014.

In 2017, there was a referendum in Iraq. A boundary was drawn, a vote was taken, and Kirkuk was in a majority Kurdish zone. If, however, that boundary had been drawn to create a more easterly region, Kirkuk could have been part of a mainly Shi'a zone. And if westerly, it could have been predominantly Sunni. As in the Balkans and the Caucasus, so today in Iraq, the right of self-determination is a recipe for conflict. And yet, in Resolution 47 passed in 1949, the United Nations decided that the dispute in Kashmir was to be resolved by a referendum. Thank heavens it has not happened!

2.3. Rwanda

In the 1930s, the colonial authorities in Rwanda decided to issue ID cards, so everyone was classified as either a Tutsi, if they were tall, or a Hutu, if small. A third ethnic group, the Twa, was ignored. Those of an average height were asked another binary question: "Do you have 10 or more cows?" (Reader, 1998: 616). If 'yes', they were Tutsi; if 'no', Hutu. So it was that a form of minority rule was established: the Hutu were the workers at the bottom of the pyramid; then came the Tutsi, the middle class; and the Europeans were on top. After WWII, the white man changed his mind: minority rule was to be replaced by majority rule, so the losers of yesterday could be the winners of tomorrow. Little wonder then that when the *Interahamwe* launched its genocide in 1994, the slogan they used was "*Rubanda Nyamwinshi*, we are the majority people." (Prunier, 1995: 183).

2.4. China

Although he didn't organize any referendums, MáoZédông was also a majoritarian. "Throughout the whole movement," said MáoZédông in 1964, "we must... win over the majority, oppose and smash the minority," (Schram, 1969: 325).

2.5. Majority Coalitions

In 2017 in Britain, the Tory Party retained power by forming a majority coalition with the Democratic Unionist Party. Two years earlier, in Israel, the Likud Party formed a majority coalition of just one seat with the Jewish Home. In both, therefore, the extremist tail is thus able to wag the dog, and hence yet more settlements on the West Bank, for example. At the same time, the Arab List knows that they are unlikely to be invited into government, ever. Just as, in Turkey, the Kurds will in all probability never be part of a majority coalition in Ankara.

2.6. Majority Rule

Majority voting, then, allows those in power to have too much power: in numerous instances, a single individual is elected to be leader. In the most primitive form of majority rule, a single-party version as in the USA, Mr. Trump then chooses his acolytes to thus dominate the political agenda, and but for a few checks and balances, the system is little more than an elected dictatorship, to use a phrase first coined in the UK by Lord Hailsham.

3. PREFERENTIAL VOTING

Now in theory, it is possible to identify the collective will if each voter expresses his/her individual will with a fair degree of accuracy; of which, more in a moment. It is therefore impossible to identify the will of the people (or the will of parliament) if some of the people (or MPs) are only saying what they *don't* like, that is, if some are voting only 'no'. If however everyone states what they do want – I want 'x', you want 'y', she wants 'z' or whatever – then it should be possible to identify the option which is the most popular.

Furthermore, in a pluralist democracy, a debate on any contentious problem should allow for the existence of more than two options. After all, there are more than two ways of drafting a constitution, of drawing up a budget, of designing a transport system, and so on. Accordingly, rather than allowing some dictator or political leader to dictate the agenda and choose the question to be put on the ballot paper, (see para. 1), the democratic process should enable all concerned to participate in drawing up a short list of, say, between four to six options.

3.1. An Analysis

So what happens when the citizenry in referendums (or MPs in parliament) are enabled to cast their preferences? How should these preferences be analysed?

Consider, then, 14 voters making a decision on the basis of four options, ***A, B, C*** and ***D***, and all with preferences as shown in Table I. On the face of it, it would seem that option ***D*** probably best represents the collective will; after all, it is the 1st or 2nd preference of every voter, albeit the 1st of only 2. But what happens when this voters' profile is analysed under different methodologies?

Table I: A voters' profile

Preferences	***14 voters***			
	5 voters	***4 voters***	***3 voters***	***2 voters***
1st preference	*A*	*B*	*C*	*D*
2nd preference	*D*	*D*	*D*	*C*
3rd preference	*C*	*C*	*B*	*B*
4th preference	*B*	*A*	*A*	*A*

In a plurality vote, only the 1st preferences are taken into consideration, so the winner is option ***A*** with a score of 5. In a two-round system of voting, TRS, if no one option gets a majority – in this example, a score of 8 or more – the two leading options from the first round plurality vote go into a second round majority vote. If, then, everyone's preferences stay the same, the winner is now option ***B*** with a score of 9.

The alternative vote, AV,[1] is a series of plurality votes, the least popular option being eliminated at each stage. So, in stage (i), the least popular, option ***D*** is out, and its 2 votes are transferred to the option which got their 2nd preference, in this instance ***C***. So the score in stage (ii) is ***A*** 5, ***B*** 4 and ***C*** 5, which means option ***B*** has now lost, so its 4 votes go (not to ***D***, which is no longer in contention but) to ***C***, so ***C*** is now the winner, again with as score of 9.

In a BC points system, as shown in Table II, all the preferences cast by all the voters are taken into consideration.

[1] Known as instant run-off voting, IRV, and preference voting, PV, in the Americas and Australasia. In Europe, when used as an electoral system rather than as a decision-making, it is sometimes called the single transferable vote, STV.

Table II: A preferential point's analysis

Preferences	***14 voters***			
	5 voters	***4 voters***	***3 voters***	***2 voters***
1st preference = 4 points	*A*= 20	*B*= 16	*C*= 12	*D*= 8
2nd preference = 3 points	*D*= 15	*D*= 12	*D*= 9	*C*= 6
3rd preference = 2 points	*C*= 10	*C*= 8	*B*= 6	*B*= 4
4th preference = 1 point	*B*= 5	*A*= 4	*A*= 3	*A*= 2

So, ***A*** gets 20 + 4 + 3 + 2 = 29

B gets 16 + 6 + 4 + 5 = 31

C gets 12 + 6 + 10 + 8 = 36

And ***D*** gets 8 + 15 + 12 + 9 = 44

The winner, now, is option ***D***.

The outcome, therefore, as shown in Table III, the totally democratic choice of all the 14 voters, is either ***A*** or ***B*** or ***C*** or ***D***.

Table III: The democratic choice

VOTING SYSTEM	***Social choice***	***Social Rankings 1st – 2nd – 3rd – 4th***	***Social Ranking Scores 1st – 2nd – 3rd – 4th***
Plurality Voting	*A*	*A-B-C-D*	*A* 5, *B* 4, *C* 3, *D* 2
TRS	*B*	*B-A*	*B* 9, *A* 5
AV	*C*	*C-A*	*B* 9, *A* 5
BC	*D*	*D-C-B-A*	*D* 44, *C* 36, *B* 31, *A* 29

At the beginning of this analysis, it was suggested that option ***D*** best represents the collective will. But only the BC gives this correct answer. Not only that: the social ranking produced with plurality voting is the complete opposite of that obtained with a points BC analysis. This and countless other examples shows that plurality/majority voting can indeed be hopelessly inaccurate, whereas a points analysis is invariably more precise.[2]

3.2. Preferential Voting

In practice, in an MBC ballot of let us say five options, if someone casts just one preference, this favourite option of his gets just 1 point.[3] Another voter who casts two preferences gives her favourite 2 points (and her 2nd preference 1 point). And so on. So he who casts all five preferences gives his favourite 5 points, (his 2nd choice 4 points, and so on). The difference between the number of points awarded to the voter's 1st and 2nd preference is always 1 point; there is no especial weighting.

So the voter would be well advised to cast all five options. At the same time, the protagonist will want her supporters to give her option their full 5 points, so she will probably try to persuade any supporters to do just that, to cast full ballots. Furthermore, she will know that success depends on getting a lot of high preferences, a few middle ones perhaps, but very few low ones. It would be worth her while, therefore, to campaign positively with

[2] One other voting methodology deserves a mention: the Condorcet rule. Like the BC, it too takes all preferences cast into consideration. And as in a BC, the voter may cast a full slate of preferences. In a Condorcet analysis of the voters' profile shown in Table I, option A is first compared with option B, and B is the more popular. Then A is compared with C, and so on. The option which wins the most pairings is the Condorcet winner. In the above example, the social choice is option D, and, as in a BC, the Condorcet social ranking is also D-C-B-A.

[3] In a ballot on n options, a voter may cast m preferences where $n \geq m \geq 1$. In a BC, points are awarded to (1st, 2nd ... last) preferences cast according to the rule:

$$(n, n-1 \dots 1) \text{ or } (n-1, n-2 \dots 0)$$

In an MBC, points are awarded as per the rule:

$$(m, m-1 \dots 1)$$

If people cast all their preferences, there is no difference at all in the outcome. If some voters truncate their ballots, however, the difference can be huge. Indeed, in the worst case scenario, if everyone casts just a 1st preference, a BC morphs into a plurality vote, which Jean-Charles de Borda bitterly opposed.

her erstwhile opponents, so to get a 4th or even a 3rd preference rather than a 5th.

Let us assume that the five options concern tax rates, and that therefore all five can be put into a sequence, from low to high or whatever: 40%, 45%, 50%, 55% and 60%. In this case, the first voter – Mr J – who casts a 1st preference (5 points) for 40% would logically have a 2nd preference of 45% (4 points), and so on, as shown in Table IV.

Table IV: Mr J's Preferences

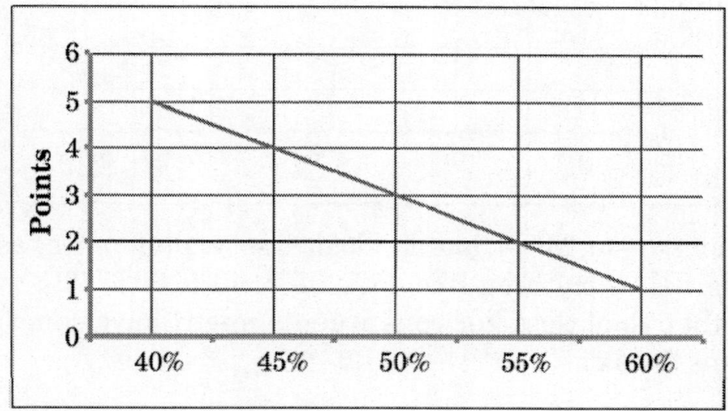

Table V: Mr J's and Ms K's Preferences

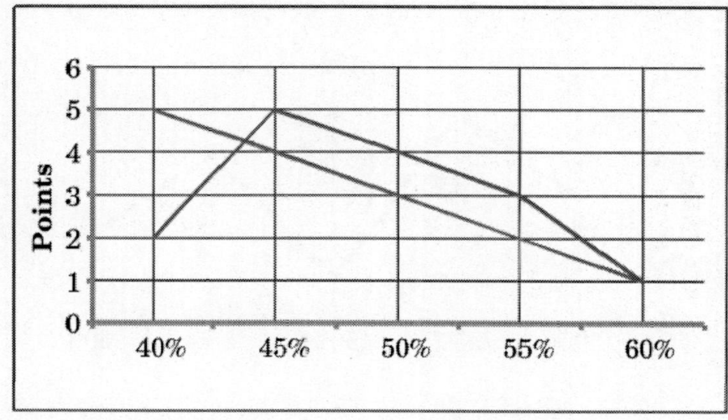

At the same time, Ms K, whose 1st preference is 45% (5 points), might have a 2nd preference of 50% (4 points), a 3rd of 55% (3 points), and so on, as shown in Table V while Mr L, whose preference is 50%, might opt for a 2nd preference of 55%, a 3rd of 45%, and so on, as in Table VI.

Table VI: Mr J's, Ms K's and Mr L's Preferences

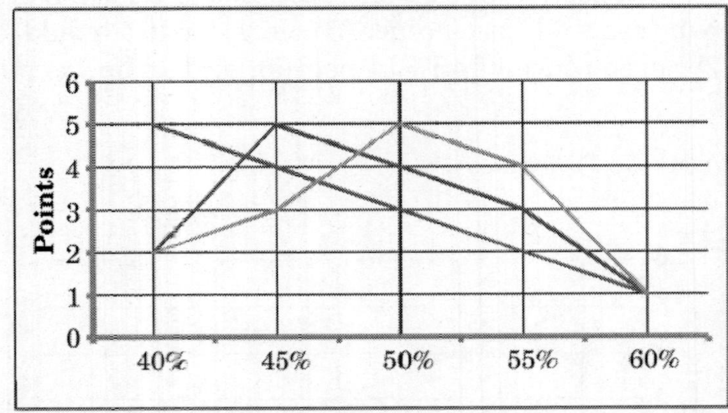

If another person, Ms M, has an illogical set of preferences as shown in Table VII, something like 45%, 55%, 40%, 60% 50% with two peaks, then doubtless her constituents might have some serious questions to ask.

Table VII: An illogical set of preferences

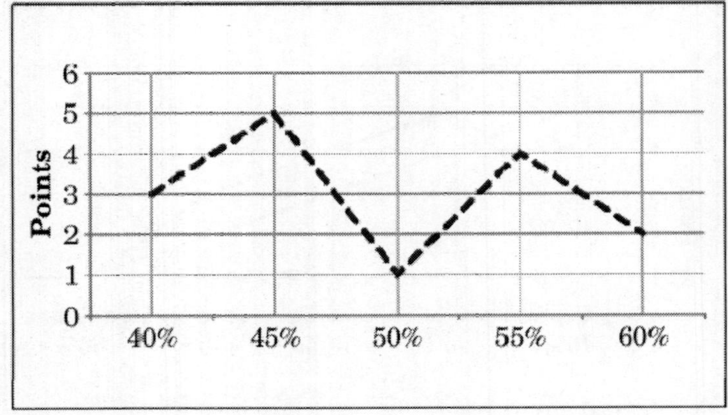

But if everyone does indeed have a logical set of preferences, then the collective will – the collection or addition of all the individual voters' points, will also be logical... always. And in this example of Mr J, Ms K and Mr L, as shown in Table VIII, the collective will is midway between 45% and 50%, that is, 47.5%.

Table VIII: The collective will

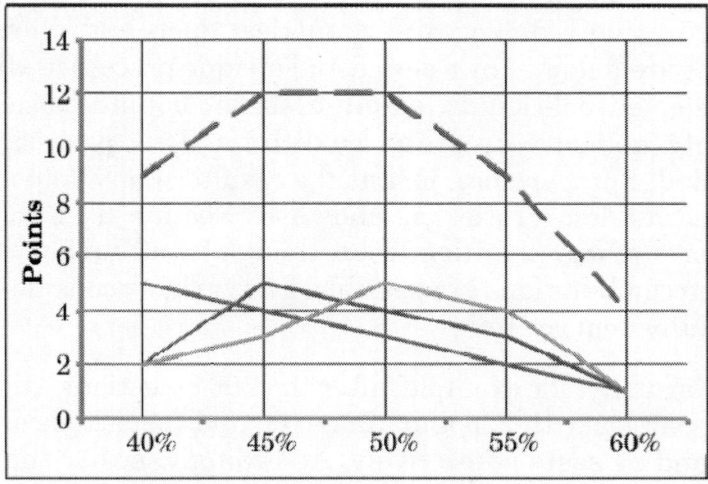

Just as it is possible to accurately determine a collective will in this way, so too the individual can express a fairly precise individual will. He who wants to support a tax rate of 50% might cast preferences for 50%, 55%, 45%, 40% and 60%, that is, evenly balanced either side of 50%. While she who would prefer 52% might cast 50%, 55%, 60%, 45%, 40%, that is, loaded to the right of 50% And so on. The degree of accuracy that can be achieved with preference voting, especially when the electorate is in the hundreds or more, can be considerable.

4. AN INCLUSIVE POLITY

An MBC, then, is more accurate, and therefore more democratic, than any majority vote. It is also non-majoritarian. It can identify the option with the highest average preference and an average, of course, involves everyone who votes, not just a majority of them. If the MBC were to be adopted as the international democratic norm, there would be no further justification for majority rule... anywhere: not the single party form of majority rule, as in the USA; and not the majority coalition form, as is often the case in continental Europe.

The present situation is often little short of bizarre. As noted earlier, in many democratic countries, open and transparent elections are followed by a closed and opaque process in which the newly-elected politicians, as often as not behind closed doors, negotiate majority or grand coalitions. This process can be protracted. Furthermore, just as the results of any vote are often regarded as democratic, (as shown in Section 3.1), so too the emergence of *any* coalition, even though in a multi-party state umpteen combinations are possible, is invariably considered to be only totally democratic.

In Germany, for example, after the 2005 elections, there were two big parties with 226 and 222 seats, and three little ones with 61, 54 and 51 seats respectively. Accordingly, either the two big parties in a grand coalition could achieve a 308 seat majority, or it could be done by a combination of either one big plus two small parties forming a majority coalition; of the latter, there were six possible combinations. Accordingly, there were seven possible minimum coalitions, each of which was, apparently, totally democratic.

There have been many other somewhat bizarre consequences. In India for example, in 1998, there was a coalition of 41 different parties. In Belgium in 2010/11, it took the parliament 451 days to sort out an administration... by which time, of course, it was almost time for the next election! While in Afghanistan, where a very large percentage of the MPs have no party affiliation, this system of democracy is almost unworkable.

In an inclusive polity, in contrast, the people would elect the parliament, hopefully by a system of PR; and then the parliament would elect the government, again by a system of PR. The appropriate methodology is called a matrix vote, but first, a word on an inclusive electoral system, the quota Borda system, QBS.

4.1. An Inclusive Electoral System

As noted above, the MBC is an inclusive decision-making procedure. The voter is encouraged by the very mathematics of the count to cast a full slate of preferences, and likewise, the protagonists are incentivised to talk positively with their erstwhile adversaries.

The MBC, however, is not proportional; so hence QBS (Emerson, 2007: 41). The election is best held in six-seater constituencies and, as in an MBC, the voters may cast a full slate of six preferences. In the count, those candidates who get a quota of high preferences are deemed elected; and then, if no further candidates reach the quota but if seats are still to be filled, those with good MBC scores get elected.

Now in a six-seater constituency, any party which thinks it has two quotas of voters can expect two candidates to be elected. If, however, that party nominates four candidates, then maybe each of these candidates gets only half a quota, and thus the party will be unsuccessful, if but at this stage of the count. Accordingly, any party will limit the number of candidates it nominates to a realistic number. Likewise, in any conflict zone, those of a particular ethno-religious group in society will also be well advised to limit the number of candidates.

At the same time, the MBC element encourages the voter to submit a full ballot. In this way, QBS encourages the voter to cross at least the gender and party divides, if not indeed any sectarian chasm.

4.2. The Matrix Vote

When parliament elects a government, it will want to choose not only a good Prime Minister but also, perhaps, a gifted Minister of Agriculture, a talented Minister of Foreign Affairs, and so on. The job specifications vary considerably, and he/she who might be qualified for one portfolio may not necessarily fit the bill in another.

Accordingly, a matrix vote enables the members of parliament to choose, in order of preference, not only those of their fellow MPs whom they want to be in government, but also the particular portfolio in which they wish each of their nominees to serve (Emerson, 2016: 79 *et seq*). A very simple sample ballot paper, as if for the election of a six-member cabinet, is shown in Table IX.

The analysis is done in two phases. First, a QBS analysis of the preferences cast identifies the six most popular candidates, and they shall form the cabinet. Then an MBC analysis of the points cast in the matrix itself identifies the particular portfolio to which each of these successful candidates shall be appointed.

Table IX: A Matrix Vote Ballot

	Preferences Names	***Prime Minister***	***Minister of Finance***	***Minister of Defence***	***Minister of Home Affairs***	***Minister of Foreign Affairs***	***Minister of Education***
1st							
2nd							
3rd							
4th							
5th							
6th							

Table X: A completed ballot

	Preferences Names	***Prime Minister***	***Minister of Finance***	***Minister of Defence***	***Minister of Home Affairs***	***Minister of Foreign Affairs***	***Minister of Education***
1st	Ms T		✓				
2nd	Mr F			✓			
3rd	Mr P						✓
4th	Ms A	✓					
5th	Ms N					✓	
6th	Ms R				✓		

So, when submitting a ballot, each MP first chooses six of his/her fellow MPS, puts them in order of preference in the shaded column, and then places a tick opposite each nominee in the appropriate column. A full ballot, as shown in Table X, will have one tick in each column, and one in each row.

In this ballot, then, Ms T gets one 1st preference for the QBS ballot, and then 6 points for the Ministry of Finance in the MBCanalysis. Mr F gets a 2nd preference and 5 points for the Ministry of Defence, and so on. The outcome of a matrix vote[4] is invariably an all-party power-sharing cabinet or a government of national unity, in which every party is represented in its proportional due, and in which every minister is well suited to the chosen portfolio.

A party with, say, 20% of the seats in parliament may expect about 20% of the seats in cabinet. The QBS element of the matrix vote incentivises each party to limit the number of its nominees to a realistic level, while the MBC part encourages each MP to cast a full ballot. Accordingly, each MP should best cross the party divide if not also any ethno-religious divide. The matrix vote, therefore, could be part of any peace process.

5. CONCLUSION

In an inclusive democracy, both the parliament and the cabinet should work in consensus, either verbally or *via* an MBC ballot. If on any one topic there is no consensus, if the option with the highest average preference is only just above the mean, then obviously, all the other options must have a similar level of support, in which case no decision should be taken and the debate should be resumed. If the option does pass a certain pre-determined threshold, however, that decision may be implanted.

[4] A matrix vote could also be used by both or all parties concerned in a majority coalition, or by the MPs of a single party in a single-party form of majority rule. A matrix vote could also be used in civil society, when association members elect an executive committee, for example.

The MPs talk together; vote together; and then work together, to ensure that the democratic will of parliament, which in a representative democracy should approximate to the democratic will of the people, is then implemented. In other words, in an inclusive polity, all MPs would share a collective responsibility to ensure the country is well run for the benefit of all. There might be those of an extreme bent who find this difficult or even impossible... and who therefore resign in the short term or, in the longer term, fail to get re-elected.

At a time when Europe is faced with an increasing number of extremist parties, it is quite extraordinary that so many people continue to believe in and use a majoritarian form of governance. It is as if they have forgotten that, not too long ago, a certain extremist came to power by means of a weighted majority vote: Adolf Hitler.

Peter Emerson
The de Borda Institute
Istanbul, 11.11.2017

REFERENCES

Deutscher, I. (1982). Stalin. Pelican. Harmondsworth.
Emerson, P. (2007). *Designing an All-Inclusive Democracy*. Springer, Heidelberg.
2012. *Defining Democracy*. Springer, Heidelberg.
2016. *From Majority Rule to Inclusive Politics*. Springer, Heidelberg.
Prunier, G. (1995). *The Rwanda Crisis*. C. Hurst and Co. London.
Reader, J. (1998). Africa. Penguin. London.
Schram, S. (1969). *The Political Thought of Mao Tse-tung*. Frederick A Praeger. New York.
deSte Croix, G.E.M. (2005). *Athenian Democratic Origins*. OUP, Oxford.

ABBREVIATIONS

AV: Alternative Vote; BC: Borda Count; IRV: Instant Run-off Voting; MBC: Modified BC; OUP: Oxford University Press; PR: Proportional Representation; PV: Preferential Voting; QBS: Quota Borda System; STV: Single Transferable Vote; TRS: Two Round System.

3

Totalitarianism, Surveillance and State of "Orwellianism": The Need for Individual Rights and True Form of Liberal Democracy

Tamanna Khosla[1]*

ABSTRACT

The present state of world has become largely Orwellian. If one were to unearth it would seem more totalitarian than democratic. The adjective Orwellian connotes an attitude and a policy of control by propaganda, surveillance, misinformation, denial of truth, and manipulation of the past. In Nineteen Eighty-Four Orwell described a totalitarian government that controlled thought by controlling language, making certain ideas literally unthinkable. Noam Chomsky too emphasized on the problem of surveillance in contemporary US. Most states are bearing the burden of surveillance which effects right to privacy of its citizens whether US, China, India or any other nation state.

Kew words: Surveillance, US, George Orwell, Whistle blowers, Snowden, Totalitarianism, Privacy, India.

[1] Department of Political Science, Delhi College of Arts and Commerce, Delhi University

**Corresponding E-mail*: tamannakhosla@gmail.com

The present state of world has become largely Orwellian. If one were to unearth it would seem more totalitarian than democratic The adjective Orwellian connotes an attitude and a policy of control by propaganda, surveillance, misinformation, denial of truth, and manipulation of the past. In Nineteen Eighty-Four Orwell described a totalitarian government that controlled thought by controlling language, making certain ideas literally unthinkable. Several words and phrases from Nineteen Eighty-Four have entered popular language. Newspeak is a simplified and obfuscatory language designed to make independent thought impossible. Double think means holding two contradictory beliefs simultaneously. The Thought Police are those who suppress all dissenting opinion. Orwell emphasized that superficial literature, film and music, used to control and indoctrinate the populace through docility. Big Brother is a supreme dictator who watches everyone[1].

A HISTORY OF MASS SURVEILLANCE

"By the early decades of the twentieth century, the US Bureau of Investigation — the precursor of today's FBI — was using wiretaps, along with mail monitoring and informants, to clamp down on those opposed to American government policies"[2].

"No matter the specific techniques involved, historically mass surveillance has had several constant attributes. Initially, it is always the country's dissidents and marginalized who bear the brunt of the surveillance, leading those who support the government or are merely apathetic to mistakenly believe they are immune. And history shows that the mere existence of a mass surveillance apparatus, regardless of how it is used, is in itself sufficient to stifle dissent. A citizenry that is aware of always being watched quickly becomes a compliant and fearful one". "Frank Church's mid - 1970s investigation into the FBI's spying shockingly

[1]George Orwell, Nineteen Eighty Four, London, 1948

[2]Glenn Grenwald's book, "No Place To Hide – Edward Snowden, The NSA, & The US Surveillance State." metropolitan books, 2014.

found that the agency had labeled half a million US citizens as potential "subversives," routinely spying on people based purely on their political beliefs. (The FBI's list of targets ranged from Martin Luther King to John Lennon, from the women's liberation movement to the anti-Communist John Birch Society)".

"On the contrary, mass surveillance is a universal temptation for any unscrupulous power. And in every instance, the motive is the same: suppressing dissent and mandating compliance".

"At the turn of the twentieth century, the British and French empires both created specialized monitoring departments to deal with the threat of anticolonialist movements".

"The ability to eavesdrop on people's communications vests immense power in those who do it. And unless such power is held in check by rigorous oversight and accountability, it is almost certain to be abused. Expecting the US government to operate a massive surveillance machine in complete secrecy without falling prey to its temptations runs counter to every historical example and all available evidence about human nature"[3].

How do governments silence whistle-blowers?[4]

"The two most favored lines of whistle - blower demonization — "he's unstable" and "he's naive" " Demonizing the personality of anyone who challenges political power has been a long-standing tactic used by Washington, including by the media. One of the first and perhaps most glaring examples of that tactic was the Nixon administration's treatment of Pentagon Papers whistle-blower Daniel Ellsberg, which included breaking into the office of Ellsberg's psychoanalyst to steal Ellsberg's files and pry into his sexual history."

---

[3]http://www.simoleonsense.com/snowden-the-nsa-and-the-u-s-surveillance-state/

[4]ibid

"The same tactic was used to damage Julian Assange's reputation well before he was accused of sex crimes by two women in Sweden. Notably, the attacks on Assange were carried out by the same newspapers that had worked with him and had benefited from Chelsea Manning's disclosures, which Assange and WikiLeaks had enabled"[5].

Casting Assange as crazy and delusional became a staple of US political discourse generally and The New York Times tactics specifically".

"The Times also led the way on the Manning coverage, insisting that what drove Manning to become a massive whistle-blower was not conviction or conscience but personality disorders and psychological instability".

"Attributing dissent to personality disorders is hardly an American invention. Soviet dissidents were routinely institutionalized in psychological hospitals, and Chinese dissidents are still often forcibly treated for mental illness".

"There are obvious reasons for launching personal attacks on critics of the status quo. As noted, one is to render the critic less effective: few people want to align themselves with someone crazy or weird. Another is deterrence: when dissidents are cast out of society and demeaned as emotionally imbalanced, others are given a strong incentive not to become one".

The administration had waged what people across the political spectrum were calling an unprecedented war on whistle-blowers. The president, who had campaigned on a vow to have the "most transparent administration in history," specifically pledging to protect whistleblowers, whom he hailed as "noble" and "courageous," had done exactly the opposite".

"Obama's administration has prosecuted more government leakers under the Espionage Act of 1917 — a total of seven—than

[5]ibid

all previous administrations in US history combined: in fact, more than double that total. The Espionage Act was adopted during World War I to enable Woodrow Wilson to criminalize dissent against the war, and its sanctions are severe: they include life in prison and even the death penalty".

"Just weeks before my arrival in Hong Kong, it was revealed that the Obama Justice Department had obtained a court order to read through the emails and telephone records of reporters and editors from the Associated Press to find their source for a story".

"Almost immediately after that, a new report revealed an even more extreme attack on the news-gathering process: the Department of Justice had filed a court affidavit accusing Fox News Washington bureau chief James Rosen of being a "co-conspirator" in his source's alleged crimes, on the grounds that the journalist had "aided and abetted" the source's disclosure of classified information by working with him closely to receive the materials".

You'd basically be instructed not to worry about it," he said. He developed a reputation among colleagues as someone who raised too many concerns, a trait that did not endear him to superiors".

"But then it became clear that Obama was not just continuing, but in many cases expanding these abuses," he said. "I realized then that I couldn't wait for a leader to fix these things. Leadership is about acting first and serving as an example for others, not waiting for others to act".

"The stuff I saw really began to disturb me," Snowden said. "I could watch drones in real time as they surveilled the people they might kill. You could watch entire villages and see what everyone was doing. I watched NSA tracking people's Internet activities as they typed. I became aware of just how invasive US surveillance capabilities had become. I realized the true breadth of this system. And almost nobody knew it was happening".

"The true measurement of a person's worth isn't what they say they believe in, but what they do in defense of those beliefs," he said. "If you're not acting on your beliefs, then they probably aren't real".

"What keeps a person passive and compliant," he explained, "is fear of repercussions, but once you let go of your attachment to things that don't ultimately matter — money, career, physical safety — you can overcome that fear".

Further Newspapers like Washington posts excessive closeness to the government, reverence for the institutions of the national security state, routine exclusion of dissenting voices. The paper's own media critic, Howard Kurtz, had documented in 2004 how the paper had systematically amplified pro-war voices in the run-up to the invasion of Iraq while downplaying or excluding opposition. The post was largely one sided in terms of reporting against Iraq.

The 2008 FISA Amendments Act is the current governing law for NSA surveillance". "The documents left no doubt that the NSA was equally involved in economic espionage, diplomatic spying, and suspicionless surveillance aimed at entire populations".

"The US government had built a system that has as its goal the complete elimination of electronic privacy worldwide. Far from hyperbole, that is the literal, explicitly stated aim of the surveillance state: to collect, store, monitor, and analyze all electronic communication by all people around the globe".

"Internet companies to provide access to all the communications of any non-American, including those with US persons — Facebook chats, Yahoo! emails, Google searches". Point was clear: if you can never evade the watchful eyes of a supreme authority, there is no choice but to follow the dictates that authority imposes. You cannot even consider forging your own path beyond those rules: if you believe you are always being watched and judged, you are not really a free individual".

"All oppressive authorities—political, religious, societal, parental — rely on this vital truth, using it as a principal tool to enforce orthodoxies, compel adherence, and quash dissent". "What made the Internet so appealing was precisely that it afforded the ability to speak and act anonymously, which is so vital to individual exploration. For that reason, it is in the realm of privacy where creativity, dissent, and challenges to orthodoxy germinate".

"What makes a surveillance system effective in controlling human behavior is the knowledge that one's words and actions are susceptible to monitoring". But mass surveillance kills dissent in a deeper and more important place as well: in the mind, where the individual trains him - or herself to think only in line with what is expected and demanded".

"History leaves no doubt that collective coercion and control is both the intent and effect of state surveillance".

"White and Zimbardo noted in their conclusion that the "threat or actuality of government surveillance may psychologically inhibit freedom of speech". They added that while their "research design did not allow for the possibility of 'avoiding assembly,'" they expected that "the anxiety generated by the threat of surveillance would cause many people to totally avoid situations".

Surveillance cheerleaders essentially offer only one argument in defense of mass surveillance: it is only carried out to stop terrorism and keep people safe. Indeed, invoking an external threat is a historical tactic of choice to keep the population submissive to government powers".

"That same month, Obama's hand-picked advisory panel (composed of, among others, a former CIA deputy director and a former White House aide, and convened to study the NSA program through access to classified information) concluded that the metadata program "was not essential to preventing attacks and could readily have been obtained in a timely manner using conventional [court] orders".

"The record is indeed quite poor. The collect-it-all system did nothing to detect, let alone disrupt, the 2012 Boston Marathon bombing. It did not detect the attempted Christmas-day bombing of a jetliner over Detroit, or the plan to blow up Times Square, or the plot to attack the New York City subway system — all of which were stopped by alert bystanders or traditional police powers. It certainly did nothing to stop the string of mass shootings from Aurora to Newtown. Major international attacks from London to Mumbai to Madrid proceeded without detection, despite involving at least dozens of operatives".

"In fact, mass surveillance has had quite the opposite effect: it makes detecting and stopping terror more difficult. Democratic Congressman Rush Holt, a physicist and one of the few scientists in Congress, has made the point that collecting everything about everyone's communications only obscures actual plots being discussed by actual terrorists. Directed rather than indiscriminate surveillance would yield more specific and useful information".

"American dying in a terrorist attack is infinitesimal, considerably less than the chance of being struck by lightning. John Mueller, an Ohio State University professor who has written extensively about the balance between threat and expenditures in fighting terrorism, explained in 2011: "The number of people worldwide who are killed by Muslim-type terrorists, Al Qaeda wannabes, is maybe a few hundred outside of war zones. It's basically the same number of people who die drowning in the bathtub each year." More American citizens have "undoubtedly" died "overseas from traffic accidents or intestinal illnesses," the news agency McClatchy reported, "than from terrorism".

"After the trouble-free Olympics, Stephen Walt noted in Foreign Policy that the outcry was driven, as usual, by severe exaggeration of the threat. He cited an essay by John Mueller and Mark G. Stewart in International Security for which the authors had analyzed fifty cases of purported "Islamic terrorist plots" against the United States, only to conclude that "virtually all of the perpetrators were 'incompetent, ineffective, unintelligent, idiotic, ignorant, unorganized, misguided, muddled, amateurish, dopey, unrealistic, moronic, irrational, and foolish.'" Mueller and Stewart quoted from Glenn Carle, former deputy national intelligence officer for transnational threats, who said, "We must see jihadists for the small, lethal, disjointed and miserable opponents that they are," and they noted that al-Qaeda's "capabilities are far inferior to its desires".

DEMOCRACY & PRIVACY

"A population, a country that venerates physical safety above all other values will ultimately give up its liberty and sanction any power seized by authority in exchange for the promise, no matter how illusory, of total security. However, absolute safety is itself chimeric, pursued but never obtained. The pursuit degrades those who engage in it as well as any nation that comes to be defined by it".

"While the government, *via* surveillance, knows more and more about what its citizens are doing, its citizens know less and less about what their government is doing, shielded as it is by a wall of secrecy".

"In a healthy democracy, the opposite is true. Democracy requires accountability and consent of the governed, which is only possible if citizens know what is being done in their name. The presumption is that, with rare exception, they will know everything their political officials are doing, which is why they are called public servants, working in the public sector, in public service, for public agencies. Conversely, the presumption is that the government, with rare exception, will not know anything that law-abiding citizens are doing. That is why we are called private individuals, functioning in our private capacity. Transparency is for those who carry out public duties and exercise public power. Privacy is for everyone else".

SURVEILLANCE IN INDIA

While we should be, some of the surveillance schemes in the world's largest democracy, India, are arguably in the same league. The official political motivation behind surveillance in India appears to be the government's determination to tackle terrorism in the country[6]. The 2008 Mumbai terrorist attacks were arguably a similar landmark to the 9/11 terrorist attacks in the US, and both governments officially announced their intention to carry out surveillance as a counter -terrorism measure. However, unlike in the west, terrorist attacks in India are much more common, and the National Security Adviser reported in 2008 that 800 terrorist cells were operational in the country. With India's history of major terror attacks in India over the last 25 years, it's easy for one to be persuaded that terrorism is actually a major threat to national security. He world's largest democracy, which is also one of the most corrupt countries in the world, is implementing many controversial surveillance schemes which lack transparency, accountability and adequate legal backing, and which are largely being carried out in secret. And to make matters worse, India lacks privacy legislation. Over a billion people in a democratic regime are exposed to inadequately regulated surveillance schemes, while a local surveillance industry is thriving without any checks or balances whatsoever. What will this mean for the global future of democracy?[7]

CONCLUSION

Privacy as Important for Individual Rights

The point is not the hypocrisy of those who disparage the value of

[6] Maria Xynou, Big Democracy, Big Surveillance; India's surveillance State, http://cis-india.org/internet governance/blog/big-democracy-big-surveillance-indias-surveillance-state

[7] http://cis-india.org/internet-governance/blog/big-democracy-big-surveillance-indias-surveillance-state

privacy while intensely safeguarding their own, although that is striking. It is that the desire for privacy is shared by us all as an essential, not ancillary, part of what it means to be human. We all instinctively understand that the private realm is where we can act, think, speak, write, experiment, and choose how to be, away from the judgmental eyes of others. Privacy is a core condition of being a free person'.

SUGGESTED READINGS

Orwell George (1948). Nineteen Eighty four, London.

Donner, Frank J. (1980). The Age of Surveillance: The Aims and Methods of America's Political Intelligence System, Knoph.

Chomsky Noam (2014). A Surveillance State Beyond Imagination is Being Created. https://news.ycombinator.com/item?id=7864438.

Xynou Maria (2014). Big Democracy, Big Surveillance; India's surveillance State. http://cis-indias.org/internet-governance/blog/big-democracy-big-surveillance-indias-surveillance-state

4

Global Civil Society and Democracy[1]

Tamanna Khosla[1]*

ABSTRACT

In the present postmodern times it is the times of upgradation of civil society. More than just civil society, focus now is on movements from civil society which is global in nature. Globalization in the 90's has promoted this phenomenon. The wave for democratization worldwide has given impetus to the global civil society movement Why is it important to understand global civil society.

Key words: Global civil society, Political and economic civil society movement, Key periods from 70s to 2000's.

GLOBAL CIVIL SOCIETY: DEFINATION IN PRESENT CONTEXT

In the present postmodern times it is the times of upgradation of civil society. More than just civil society, focus now is on movements from civil society which is global in nature. Globalization in the

[1] Department of Political Science, Delhi College of Arts and Commerce, Delhi University

**Corresponding E-mail*: tamannakhosla@gmail.com

[1]Republished from intellectual resonance.

90's has promoted this phenomenon. The wave for democratization worldwide has given impetus to the global civil society movement. Why is it important to understand global civil society? One of the reasons is that it gives insight into what a democratic set up would look like in current political societies. Second reason is that there is equal amount of authoritarian governments in the world with clamor for democratization from the ground example being the Chinese democratic upsurge in Tiananmen Square. Global civil society gives hope to world's oppressed people that world can have a say in their matters. The ideological focus on deliberative democracy has given impetus to global civil society movement. Thus the article argues the need for giving power to civil society to bring about changes in political, economic, social and cultural sphere.

Here we need to understand what is global civil society movement. We will also understand how deliberative democracy assists in global civil society movement.

I

The words 'global' and 'civil society' have become commonplace during the last decade. Yet what they mean and how they come together are subject to widely differing interpretations. Albrow and Seckinelgin, paraphrasing Nancy Fraser, defined global civil society as a 'dynamic of claims and counterclaims for justice that extends far beyond the discursive frame of the conventional nation state'[2].

This dynamic has been particularly pronounced in 2011, with virulent claims and counter claims pertaining to international criminal justice as well as social justice. Civil society has come to be considered as an essential component in contemporary global politics, taken either as a normative concept linked to the idea of democracy or as a descriptive concept referring to the activism of

[2] Albrow, Martin and Glasius, Marlies (2007). 'Democracy and the Possibility of a Global Public Sphere'. In: Albrow Martin et al. (ed.), Global Civil Society, London: Sage Publications, p. 1.

NGOs, social movements, and global advocacy networks. Further, from the beginning global civil society is conceived as a 'fuzzy and contested concept' with both descriptive and normative content. For operational purposes, the global civil society year book adopted an empirical definition of global civil society as 'the sphere of ideas, values, institutions, organisations, networks, and individuals located *between* the family, the state, and the market and operating *beyond* the confines of national societies, polities, and economies[3]. As the journey progressed, scholars became increasingly critical of the dominant associational notion of global civil society that is often equated with international NGOs So subsequently, social scientists began to experiment with alternative, more normative versions of the concept: communicative power, for example, or the space where justice is deliberated, or a realm of civility and non-violence. In India for example civil society movement was gives importance since time immemorial. But the prim promoter of the concept was MK Gandhi. He gave importance to people to move against violence and injustice and focus on non violence as a method for civil society movement against British. In post independent India he gave importance to villages the lowest tier to organize itself.

Further, one way in which we chose to interpret civil society is as the medium through which individuals participate in public affairs, and through which they endorse or challenge the dominant discourse. It is a constantly shifting medium – sometimes characterised by consensus and sometimes by sharp polarisation and struggle, sometimes changing slowly and sometimes, in revolutionary moments, dramatically. Its concrete manifestations – as coffee houses or market places in the eighteenth century, town hall meetings and party conferences in the twentieth century, or Facebook and tent cities most recently – vary according to time and place.

[3]Helmut Anheier, Glasius Marlies and Kaldor Mary (eds.) (2001). Global Civil Society, Oxford University Press, p. 17

Moreover the growth and expansion of global civil society as a phenomenon in the 1990s seemed closely associated with a major shift in cultural and social values that took hold in most developed market economies in the 1970s. This shift saw a change in emphasis from material security to concerns about democracy, participation and meaning, and involved, among others, a formation towards cosmopolitan values such as tolerance and respect for human rights[4]. These values facilitated the cross-national spread of social movements around common issues that escaped conventional party politics, particularly in Europe and Latin America, and led to a broad-based mobilisation in social movements, with the women's, peace, democracy and environmental movements the best examples of an increasingly international 'movement industry'[5]. Contemporary society is far more conscious of environmental and human rights and the importance of gender equality, and far more inclusive in terms of race, language, religion or sexual orientation than in 1950s and 1960s. Not only in the West, but also in growing parts of Asia and Latin America, Africa and the Middle East, today's generation are the children of the internet, the mobile phone and cheap air travel – the 'globalisation' generation. They know that the world is a singular fragile eco-system – and that while the national state does have a role to play, it is part of a broader global community. And above all, as has become so movingly obvious in Tahrir Square, on the streets of Syrian towns or even in the Yemen, most believe in non-violence as a fundamental guiding principle[6].

[4]Inglehart, R. (1990). Cultural Shift in Advanced Industrial Society. Princeton, NJ: Princeton University Press.

[5]Diani, M. and McAdam, D. (*eds.*) (2003). Social movements and networks: Relational approaches to collective action. Oxford: Oxford University Press; McAdam, D., Tarrow, S. and Tilly, C. (2001). Dynamics of Contention. New York: Cambridge University Press.

[6]Anheier, Helmut;c.it Another example that can be set forth is that in May 2011, in his speech announcing the death of Osama bin Laden, President Obama referred to the operation to shoot him and throw his body into the sea as 'an operation to get Osama bin Laden and bring him to justice' ('Osama bin Laden Killed', 2011). In New York bin Laden,

Footnotoe 6 (*Contd...*)

In particular, Western support for dictators in the region has been underpinned by orientalist assumptions about the incompatibility of Islamic societies with democracy and civil society. The protestors in Tunisia, Egypt, Syria, Yemen and elsewhere have disproved these theories. They have displayed extraordinary dignity and self-restraint. With the exception of Libya, the protestors have refused to be drawn into violence in spite of huge provocation. This determined stance in Syria, where at the time of writing, some 2,200 people have been killed, is truly inspirational. They have shown an exemplary degree of self-organisation, with people's committees springing up everywhere. They have refused to be framed as sectarian or Islamist; Muslims and Christians, Sunni and Shi'a, women in veils and women with their hair streaming behind them have stood together in Tahrir Square, Pearl Square and many other places. Like the crowds in Prague or Berlin in 1989, the protestors are showing that they can be the agents of history. However these events unfold, an active civil society has begun a movement for democracy across the region. Even Israelis have been affected by this mood of expressing indignation and taking charge of destiny: tent cities have sprung up all over Israel, inspired by Tahrir Square. The subtitle of the same yearbook suggests that global civil society can be defined as 'communicative power' as opposed to the power of force or money[7].

Footnotoe 6 (*Contd...*)

President Obama referred to the operation to shoot him and throw his body into the sea as 'An operation to get Osama bin Laden and bring him to justice' ('Osama bin Laden Killed', 2011). In New York and Washington DC thousands took to the streets to celebrate this 'justice'. In other places, including Berlin, Cairo, Istanbul, Java, Kashmir, London and different cities of Pakistan, protest demonstrations were held ('Reaction to the Death of Osama', 2011).Secondly, The trial of former Egyptian president Hosni Mubarak, and more specifically the controversial decision by the judges to stop televising the proceedings, has led to clashes between Mubarak supporters and opponents (Kirkpatrick, 2011). The trial contains elements of social justice as well as criminal justice, as Mubarak and his sons stand accused not only of responsibility for the death of demonstrators but also for corruption and illegal business deals (Shenker, 2011).

[7]Ibid;p 2

Here we would look at the types of civil society which have started in 2000's.

II TYPES OF GLOBAL CIVIL SOCIETY MOVEMENTS

Political Reforms: Emphasis on democratization worldwide against non-democratic government's Political movements worldwide have been focusing on democratization worldwide by people. We need to see how these movements have expanded from one state to another. Popular focus on democratization has expanded. From 2010 onwards there were several movements which spoke about the need for political reforms in world. The attempt was to bring more democratization in world. The world oldest democracy US saw the need for more transparency in the democratic process. Wikileaks released confidential documents on the war in Afghanistan, Iraq and Guantanamo base, to newspapers.

Similarly in 2010, in Tunisia, a vegetable salesman action sparks huge protests in Tunisia, and marks the start of the 'Arab Spring'. President Ben Ali flees the country as protest from civil society forced him to do so. In Syria there were protests against the regime of President Bashar al-Assad[8].

In 2011, the people of southern Sudan vote in a referendum for independence. The Republic of South Sudan is declared an independent state.

In Libya following a Day of Rage in Benghazi against the regime of Colonel Qadhafi, protests spread across the country. Qadhafi refuses to step down and the country plunges into civil war, with citizens taking over the running of all public services in the Benghazi area.

In Egypt huge protests in Cairo and elsewhere against the regime of Hosni Mubarak. After a series of crackdowns and the subsequent occupation of Tahrir Square, the president resigns.

[8]Ibid;p 3

Further in, Italy thousands of Italian women protest against the chauvinism of President Silvio Berlusconi, marching in more than 60 towns and cities across Italy, and as far away as Tokyo. In a referendum in 2011, Italians vote against immunity for cabinet ministers, in a move seen as an attack on Berlusconi's future.

In 2010, China arrested and imprisoned in 2008 for authoring the Charter 08 manifesto, which demanded democratic reform and an end to the one-party system. Liu Xiaobo was awarded the 2010 Nobel Prize. This caused a diplomatic row and immediate censorship of the announcement by Chinese government which was however hailed worldwide.

In Swaziland, Pro-democracy rallies are held in Africa's last absolute monarchy. Further in particular, Western support for dictators in the west Asia region has been underpinned by orientalist assumptions about the incompatibility of Islamic societies with democracy and civil society. But this has been resisted by people and organized civil society. The protestors in Tunisia, Egypt, Syria, Yemen and elsewhere have disproved these theories by westerners. They have displayed extraordinary dignity and self-restraint. With the exception of Libya, the protestors have refused to be drawn into violence in spite of huge provocation. They have shown an exemplary degree of self-organization, with people's committees springing up everywhere. They have refused to be framed as sectarian or Islamist, Muslims and Christians, Sunni and Shi'a. Women in veils and women with their hair streaming behind them have stood together in Tahrir Square, Pearl Square and many other places. Like the crowds in Prague or Berlin in 1989, the protestors are showing that they can be the agents of history[9].

However these events unfold, an active civil society has begun a movement for democracy across the region. Even Israelis have been affected by this mood of expressing indignation and taking charge of destiny: tent cities have sprung up all over Israel, inspired

[9]Ibid;p 5

by Tahrir Square. Although focused primarily on social demands, these tent city protests could have implications for the peace process as the demonstrators, who include both Jewish and Arab Israelis, make the point of contrasting the huge settlement programme in the Palestinian territories with inadequate social housing inside Israel. In an era of globalisation, where it is almost impossible to sustain closed societies, authoritarian states depend on consent. When that consent is withdrawn they cannot survive. They can, however, try to reproduce consent through the mobilisation of fear, and this leads not to stability but to anarchy, lawlessness and violence.

In analyses of the Arab Spring, there has been much attention to the extent to which the use of Facebook, Twitter and social media allowed immediate diffusion of information about mobilisation and repression. This was profoundly important. But equally important was the role of satellite television channels in Arabic, particularly al-Jazeera, which disseminated information picked up from social networking sites. These transnational Arabic channels have already contributed to an emerging pan-Arabic civil society and, by the same token, their role in the revolutions has enormously enhanced their status and popularity. The communications aspect of the Arab revolts could also be understood as part of a wider global civil society trend of simultaneously utilising and demanding transparency against secretive or corrupt organisations, not just in authoritarian settings and not just at the state level. Wikileaks is a prime example in this context: while it has existed and posted classified information since 2006, Wikileaks shot to fame in April 2010, when it showed a video of a 2007 US airstrike on Baghdad in which journalists were mistakenly fired at[10].

Further global civil society is also defined as 'the medium through which the consciousness and perceptions of risk are shaped and new methods of protection are promoted'[11]. This aspect of global civil society was clearly demonstrated in the rapid

[10]Ibid;p 8

[11]Ibid;p 1

change of views on nuclear power after the radioactive leakage from the Fukushima plant caused by the Tohoku earthquake in Japan in March 2011. In Italy, the return to nuclear power was overwhelmingly rejected in a referendum, and in Germany and Switzerland nuclear power is being phased out[12] (Faris, 2011). Nevertheless, what these path-breaking decisions showed was that, over the long-term, social movements like the anti-nuclear movement can bring about fundamental changes in attitudes, and ultimately, policy. For example the protests that brought hundreds of thousands of people to the street in Spain, Greece, Portugal, Israel and Ireland are also about social justice: they protest against unemployment, wage cuts and other austerity measures, but beyond that also about having been lied to by politicians and being disproportionally targeted by austerity cuts while bankers were bailed out[13].

ENVIRONMENTAL MOVEMENTS: NON VIOLENCE AGAINST NATURE

Environmental movements in the last decade have got an impetus from political movements for democracy. Politicians and an oligarchy of industrialists have vested interests in exploitation of environment. Here comes the civil society which has harped on the need for protection of people against these irresponsible behavior of the nexus between politicians and industrialists.

In 2010, United States, an explosion at the BP drilling rig Deep Water Horizon results in the largest offshore oil spill in US history. International outrage ensued. Civil society groups post a letter to the US Senate urging them to reconsider off-shore drilling and over 800,000 people join the Facebook group 'Boycott BP', which, along with other mobilizations, culminates in an international day

[12] https://grahamscambler.wordpress.com/2013/01/30/habermas-civil-society-and-the-public-sphere/

[13] ibid

of protest. Even now, cleanup and litigation expected to take many years.

Also in 2010, Hungary, toxic mud is leaked from the Ajka alumina plant in the worst chemical spill in the country's history, leading to an outcry by environmental NGOs. 2010 also saw in Mexico, a coalition of civil society organisations call for a 'democratic, transparent and participatory process at the UN climate talks' at the COP16 in Cancun, but the deals that come out of the talks are critiqued as rescuing UN credibility rather than the environment.

In 2011, East Africa saw a regional food security alert from the Famine Early Warning Systems Network which joined the rising clamour of voices from NGOs and UN agencies predicting famine in East Africa. Although 'the worst drought in 60 years' was blamed, with climate change fingered as the culprit, observers also point to rising food prices, continued regional confiict, systemic poverty and the failure of states to honour aid promises. The reluctance of the UN to define a critical situation as a famine has also been criticised. The food crisis affected more than 12 million people in Djibouti, Ethiopia, Kenya, Somalia and Southern Sudan, with famine officially declared by the UN in areas of Somalia in July.

2011 saw in Germany Following the March 11 tsunami in Japan and subsequent leaks at the Fukushima nuclear plant, large protests against nuclear energy sweep across Germany and France. As a result of popular pressure, Chancellor Merkel announces that Germany will be free of nuclear energy by 2022. Subsequently, Italians vote against the resumption of their country's nuclear power programme, in a referendum held on 14 June 2010. In 2010, Pakistan Two months of abnormally heavy rains cause repeated flooding in the Indus basin. 2,000,000 people are affected – civil society rallies to organise help for the victims. 2010, also sees movement in against toxic mud leaked from the Ajka alumina plant in the worst chemical spill in the country's history, leading to an outcry by environmental NGOs.

ECONOMIC MOVEMENTS: IN FAVOR OF WELFARISM

Economic movements have gained from the socialist revolution and the need to ensure welfarism for the citizenry.

In United Kingdom for example, major protests take place in London against education cuts, the rise in university tuition fees, along with numerous smaller protests and lengthy university sit-ins that occur around the UK. 2010 saw protests in Dublin, against EU bailout and austerity measures. An estimated 100,000 take to the streets of Dublin to protest against austerity measures called for by the IMF and EU.

III GLOBAL CIVIL SOCIETY: A TRAIL FROM 1970s TO 2017

Here we will also look at the changes which have come about globally in civil society movements and the medium of these changes. It shows how the present decade focuses on democratization.

Fields	*Value changes*
1970s: Economic, research and science; INGOs (International Non-Governmental Organizations)	Humanitarian membership-based
1980s: Value-based;	INGOs linked to International Social Movement Cosmopolitan values
1990s: Value-based; service provision	Corporate and public management NGOs
2000s: Anti-capitalism; opposition to war	Social Forums
2010s: Democracy, social Justice	Web-based activism; Tweets

CRITQUE OF CIVIL SOCIETY CONCEPT

Thompson went on to object, however, that in 'The Structural Transformation of the Public Sphere' Habermas[14]:

[14]ibid

- Neglected non-bourgeois or popular forms of public discourse and activity, some of them militantly opposed to bourgeois culture and practice;
- Overlooked prior historical examples, notably at the time of the English Civil War;
- Made too little of the absence of women (as feminists have pointed out, the absence of women was constitutive of the public sphere: it was juxtaposed to the private sphere in a gender-specific way);
- Exaggerated both the precipitous nature of the decline of the public sphere and the passivity of later recipients of media products

IV CONCLUSION

Need for Deliberative Democracy

How this struggle plays out depends to a large extent to whether the newly emerging emancipatory social movements can transform themselves into a political movement. Can they develop a political agenda capable of constructing new sources of political authority with the capacity to address the big issues of our time?

The workers' movements and the anti-colonial movements of the early twentieth century provided the political basis for the strengthening of the state in the late twentieth century. The post -'68 movements had a far-reaching cultural impact and also contributed to democratisation, as well as to the consolidation of humanitarian, human rights and peacekeeping institutions at an international level. The protests of 2011 have the potential to re-instil public morality and to help build institutions at regional and global levels that can tackle such issues as global inequality (be it of wealth or concerns gender disparity) and or environmental necessity, although at present they seem largely focused on national and local levels. Already there are some largely unnoticed but significant innovations at a non-national institutional level.

The German and French leaders agreed in August 2011, for example, on a European tax on financial transactions – something long demanded by Social Forum activists. The International Monetary Fund has uncharacteristically reacted to the Arab Spring and the European sovereign debt crisis with political concerns about how to sustain social cohesion. In other words, there is what sociologists call a political opportunity structure. The next decade will be a dramatic learning process for the new global generation. Can they articulate a shared political agenda that has the potential to save their successors from the dire consequences of deprivation, climate change and war?

Thus in the current scenario the global civil society seems fixated with the idea of need of democracy and more deliberative democracy to the people. No deliberation procedure can succeed till a certain level of trust and mutual respect is established between groups, within groups and between the state and groups. A society needs to fulfil the conditions of 'minimal decency'. No group should be in a more advantageous position. A balance of power should exist between the deliberating parties. Deliberation for groups is not possible from a position of inequality.

Power needs to be transferred to the people. Good governance with focus on participation and transparency need to be practiced. Responsiveness by the states worldwide needs to be spread. Equity between people, between minorities, gender and other social, political groups need to be focus of governments. Debureaucratization is must for democracy to function to the fullest.

Thus dialogue between governments and citizenry is a must. Further contemporary problems like terrorism can also be handled better if people and global civil society are involved. Thus strengthening of civil society in the present cosmopolitan setup is a must which would lead to addressing several contemporary problems.

SUGGESTED READINGS

Albrow, Martin and Glasius, Marlies (2007-2008). *'Democracy and the Possibility of a Global Public Sphere'*, In: Albrow Martin et al. (eds.), Global Civil Society London: Sage Publications.

Helmut Anheier, Glasius Marlies and Kaldor Mary (eds) (2001). Global Civil Society, Oxford University Press.

Inglehart, R. (1990). Cultural Shift in Advanced Industrial Society. Princeton, NJ: Princeton University Press.

Diani, M. and McAdam, D. (eds.) (2003). Social movements and networks: Relational approaches to collective action. Oxford: Oxford University Press.

McAdam, D., Tarrow, S. and Tilly, C. (2001). Dynamics of Contention. New York: Cambridge University Press.

Helmut Anheier, Kaldor Mary and Glasius Marlies (2001-2011). The Global Civil Society Year Book: Lessons and Insights.

Kaldor Mary, Moore Henritta L. and Selchow Sabine (2012). Global Civil Society, Ten Years of Critical Reflection, Palgrave Macmillan.

5

The Role of Social Capital and Horizontal Relations in the Formation of Civil Society in Uzbekistan

SANJAR SH. SAIDOV[1]*

ABSTRACT

This article analyzes the social capital as the most important factor in the development of society. And also, we study the processes of formation of horizontal relations.

Key words: Social capital, Civil society, Horizontal relations, Socialization.

Nowadays it should be highly paid attention to the role and importance of social capital in society in planning the development degree and future of each country. Social capital issue is the research object of most humanitarian subjects and several conceptual views have been formed till now. Research the social capital as an independent branch began in the middle of last

[1] Senior Scientific Research-Worker of Uzbekistan State University of World Languages, Chilanzar-18, House 10a, Apt. # 5, Tashkent, 100153, Uzbekistan.

**Corresponding E-mail*: s.saidov.uz@gmail.com

century. However, the term of social capital and some searching's to which related started forming in the early XX century.

The term "social capital" was brought in the work of American researcher Lida Hanifan. According to his work social capital is firstly *"a significant situation affecting to people's daily life"*[1]. The author emphasizes friendship, mutual respect, kinship relations as such situations.

Jane Jacobs, who researched the social capital as urban life form as well as relations with neighbors, stressed that social capital appears to be consisted of different fields (сеть - networks) and principles.

Sociologist and economist Glenna Luri concluded that the role of social capital factor in current process has a large importance in the process of learning the degree of economical benefits of various nation representatives and distinction among them. In his definition social capital is "among people new knowledge and practice a system serves to form natural social relations"[2]. Later researchers paid attention to the conception of social capital and methodology of learning deeply. In 1983 Per Burdeo defined the social capital in his work as following: *"social capital is a present and possible complex including fixed branch connections based on mutual obligation and responsibility"*[3].

Besides in researching the issue of social capital J. Coulman, R. Patnem, F. Fukuyama, A. Shadrin, M. Gracebill, V. Grissaenko and others' works as well as their scientific theories are also important.

So the social capital is indivisible part of democratic processes. In society social capital expressing the relations among people and trust related to them and moral principles cover the mechanisms of social affecting. Social capital is a particular investment to consolidate social justice and trust scales in society, for the development of state and society institutions, for the formation of social attitudes and the increase of people abundance.

Although the power of social capital has been well recognised in daily life for a long time, as a social science concept it has emerged to prominence in relatively recent years. It has attracted attention for a number of reasons. In part, it represents a reaction against what is now seen as the excessive individualism of policy-makers (and voters) in the Reaganite and Thatcherite years. When Margaret Thatcher famously proclaimed, during an interview, that 'There is no such thing as society', many took this quite literally as an exhortation to unbridled individualism. Subsequently, Mrs. Thatcher tried to explain that she had simply been arguing that society was a rather abstract notion, and she preferred instead to dwell on the needs of families, individuals and local communities (Thatcher, 1993: 626–7), but no one seems to have believed her. Even though the original interview suggests that her explanation was entirely plausible, the more individualistic interpretation had already taken root. In these circumstances, new ideas about the rediscovery of the social appealed to a wider public, as well as to the policy community.

Ideas about social capital are also brought to the fore by recent changes in social behaviour and relationships. Lamentation over the decline of community has become a leitmotif of contemporary journalism. Let me consider just one example among many, which is distinctive only in that it comes from a former editor of *Marxism Today*, fresh on his return from four years in the dynamic environment of Hong Kong, rather than from a backward-looking advocate of traditional values hankering after a lost world of Victorian stability. Looking around Europe, Martin Jacques finds himself dismayed by the erosion of relationships by rampant individualism and the values of the market. Ours, he complains, is 'a world of increasing impermanence, transience and ephemerality, where little or nothing is forever, and individual gratification is the highest priority'. For many, marriage has become a short-term arrangement or even something to be avoided, while having children has become a rarity. Jacques blames what he calls 'the balkanisation of society' for such ills as a low birth rate and a faltering and broken process of socialisation of the young, and fears that there are 'dark times ahead' (Jacques, 2002: 24). Journalistic hyperbole aside, it does seem that in western societies at least, patterns of interaction are changing.

Informalisation of interpersonal relationships, the continuing erosion of habit and custom as the basis of human behaviour, the growing division of labour, the blurring of boundaries between public and private, and the explosion of new means of communication have drawn attention to the ways in which social order is maintained. The boundaries and contexts of special relationships are no longer explained or maintained by reference to rigid and formalised codes; to an increasing extent, they can be chosen, and also given up. We do not need to buy into the whole postmodernist package to accept that identity and subjectivity are not unified and given but are open to negotiation and indeterminacy, even where they are inflected by such inherited attributes as ethnicity or gender. Neither should we forget that institutionalised roles and relationships still demonstrate a remarkable degree of persistence, of course, as can be seen at their starkest in the continued inequalities of class and gender. Social capital has also benefited from the cultural turn in the social sciences.

Along with a marked rise in the attention given to the cultural aspects of social behaviour, there has been a remarkable growth of interest in what might be called the micro-level of individual behaviour and experience. A remarkable number of eminent social scientists have looked closely at intimacy and trust, to take two examples close to the heart of social capital (Beck and Beck-Gernsheim, 1994; Giddens, 1991; Jamieson, 1998; Luhmann, 1988; Misztal, 1996; and Sztompka, 1999). While most of these writers have said little about social capital as such (with the exceptions of Misztal and Stompka), their preoccupations do reflect a concern with the precise texture of day-to-day interaction and the quality of interpersonal relationships. This general context of intellectual concern provides a backdrop for the sharp rise of interest among social scientists, in particular, in social capital. Finally, social capital has acquired an uneasy relationship with economics. It has clear parallels with the notion of human capital, which originally emerged in economics during the 1960s, and denotes the economic value to firms, individuals and the wider public of such attributes as skill, knowledge and good health. In his influential account of school performance in American cities, James Coleman developed the concept of social capital as a way of integrating social theory with economic theory, claiming that social capital and human capital are generally complementary (Coleman, 1988–9).

Important official bodies like the World Bank and the Organisation for Economic Co-operation and Development have tended to share this view (OECD 2001a, 2001b; World Bank 2001). In a recent report on *The Wellbeing of Nations*, for example, the OECD argued for 'strong complementarity' between human capital and social capital, with each feeding the other in mutually beneficial ways (OECD, 2001b; 13). However, Schuller prefers to see social capital as offering an alternative to the concept of human capital, emphasising the collective where the latter sees only individuals pursuing their self-interests (Schuller, 2000). Others have even argued that the notion of social capital represents a colonisation of the social sciences by economists who recognise the limitations of too individualistic a view of human behaviour (Fine, 2000). Conceivably, the reverse is equally likely: that is, social capital might be seen as an attempt by sociologists to appropriate one of the core ideas of economics, and apply it to build a bridgehead into their neighbouring (and senior) discipline. My own view is that there is probably some truth in the second view, and that interest in social capital represents an attempt to modify the traditional focus of economists on individual behaviour, by stressing the social basis of peoples' decisions.

Social capital serves to the development for both personal and the effectiveness of social activity. In its turn, it consists of physical capital and human capital. While the physical capital is described in financed forms, human capital is difficult to feel. Because this capital is reflected in human's knowledge and skills. And social capital is impossible to feel, in other words ' to touch with hands'. This is an event based on social behavior, social intelligence.

Social capital is not a personal possession but wealth that can be used by all. It is apparent not in people's mind like human capital, in reality like financial capital or in bank accounts like economical capital but in social interactions and in the process of human socialization. In other words, any person should have a source supplying his demands by others to have social capital and in its turn, he must make social profit for another person himself. More clearly, values gathered during people's connections function as balance to conform people's activities. From this point of view, the conception of social capital is a very large notion and to realize, understand and analyze its negative sides demand plenty of researches.

It is necessary to emphasize that social capital consists of three bases:

(i) Social norms,
(ii) Social connections, and
(iii) Trust categories.

In each society there is a system of historically formed social standards and it advances with social development subsequently. These norms are put in order with moral rules defended by that society (nation).

Social relations represent, in its turn, institutionalized and in sensitive bases. While the first type includes social groups, branches, unities and laws obeyed by them, the second type includes connections among people in society, values, social life attitudes.

All fields in which exist social capital trust category plays an important role. It is fact that trust is a complex moral category and it is an attitude based on faith, right, fair and sincere belief. There can be shown several signs of trust event. First of all, trust is a moral relation among people. It is important to know each other well in trust. Trust is based on complete voluntariness. Trust carries out in a way that represents the best idea and feelings. In the society that is no trust cannot be exist mutual affecting and different forms of knowledge exchange.

HORIZONTAL RELATIONS

The societies in which social capital is developed horizontal form of social relations or horizontal social relations are formed.

Horizontal relations are firstly based on equality of values and trust. And it is a system of connections including tolerance, respect, unity of concerns, human rights. Besides, horizontal relations mean mutual association that has an opportunity to share with data; resources, ideas and feelings as well as necessity.

If we interpret more clearly, horizontal that is different from vertical relations based on hierarchical system is described in equality relations in society. In it person can obtain to show his ability and to find his own place in society.

Some researches show that the people who live in the societies which non-hierarchical and horizontal social relations are developed carry out more inventions, science and technology discoveries rather than the people who live in hierarchical societies. The reason for that may be defined with taking place the non-centralized processes, strengthening trust category, the increase of people's labour effectiveness and intensification of stimulation in country as well as the development of horizontal relations.

Horizontal relations are represented in the activity of formed social unities on the optional basis according to people's interests, views, intelligence, action, hobby and the level of life comprehension. These types of social groups can be different, in this process the factor to unify them is horizontal relations based on equality and belief.

Nowadays we may see bright samples of horizontal relations in developed Western societies. For example, more than 1 million different organizations, unions and associations are working in the United States of America. These are formed as an initiator group based on complete equality principles according to their activity and interest. They include 'Book lovers Society', 'Organization of fishermen', 'Moto bikers union', 'Anti globalists' confederation'. Current social groups work on the basis of general accepted law, rule and values in their activity. The most important thing is that horizontal social relations dominate in the group. This type of social unions don't have to be accredited by the state or act in another bureaucratic system and they operate as initiator group.

If we take a look at the experience of some developing countries, we may observe that vertical and hierarchic system dominate mostly rather than horizontal relations. For example, family is highly valued in Eastern society, definitely family is an institution reached the level of social value. But vertical relations in family and hierarchic control system may cause the decrease of individual abilities of children, having difficulty in the process of socialization and not to be able to defend his concerns.

The development of horizontal relations serves to the strengthening of social capital, the formation of citizenship society and as the base of country social development. Here the person tries not only for himself, but also for the people and society around him. It results the creation of several factors such as the social conscience and community control[4].

We refer some samples of Western countries as the proof of our words. If you drive in red light of traffic signal while you are driving in Germany, the driver behind you call to the police officer to warn that you break the rule. And in the next crossroads police officers will be waiting for you.

Or you live in a multi-storey building. It is winter. It snowed a lot and pavements are slippery. Someone fell on the ice by slipping in the area of your house. In this case you have to pay fine for the person as you did not clean the snow on the pavements in time. In Israel, if any person sees something suspicious (for example an object like explosive) while walking in the street, he must inform the police immediately. If he does not inform to the police, he is called to court. If that object is a real explosive and is neutralized by the police officers that person receives a reward in the amount of 35 percent of possible damage.

We may count such samples a lot. Most importantly, the increase of social capital and the formation of horizontal relations affect to each person's life, progress of society and future of the country positively. We may observe that the social capital is completely mixed with our national mentality. Its roots come from brightened religious-philosophical tradition over centuries, customs and culture that related to only Uzbeks. And it serves to provide the steadiness and closeness of society life, to be respected of national and humanistic values. Social capital especially represents in Uzbek tolerance and hospitability traditions.

Furthermore, it is clear that preserving historically formed social capital elements, receive its new brims for ourselves and to perform total social modernization in society finally help to build democratic government and strong citizenship society in the development of current globalization, internet and virtual social relations time.

REFERENCES

[1] Hanifan, L.J. (1916). The Rural School Community Centre. *Annals of the American Academy of Political and Social Sciences*, 67: 130–138.

[2] Loury, G.Ñ. (1976). Dynamic Theory of Racial Income Differences. *Discussion Papers*, 225.

[3] Bourdieu, P. (1985). The forms of capital. In: *Handbook of Theory and Research for the Sociology of Education*, Richardson, J.G. (*ed.*) New York: Greenwood.

[4] Татарко, À.Í and Lebedeva, N.M. (2009ã). Social capital: Theory and psychological research.

6

Factors of Changing Iran's Foreign Policy Approach of Idealism to Pragmatism: The First and Second Decade of the Islamic Revolution

HAMID SARMADI[1] AND SEYED ALIREZA AZGHANDI[2]*

ABSTRACT

This study aims at investigating the origins of Iran's foreign policy approach from idealism to pragmatism relying on comparing the first and the second decades of the Islamic Revolution by using discourse analysis. Due to the nature of the Islamic revolution and the taking over of sovereignty by the Islamists, expressing idealistic slogans and the dominance of idealism in the field of internal and external discourse in the early years of the revolution were seemed commonplace. But the war and the destruction of the Iranian economy, international situation and the isolation of the Islamic Republic of Iran in the global arena and also the circulation of political elites in 1368 and the rise of pragmatic economy –driven of Hashemi Rafsanjani, Iran's foreign policy shifted from the

[1] Political Science and Research Branch Islamic Azad University, Tehran, Iran

[2] Department of Political Science and Research Branch Islamic Azad University, Tehran, Iran

Corresponding E-mail: A.azghandi100@gmail.com

approach of idealismin the first decade of the Islamic Revolution to pragmatism in the second decade

Key words: Islamic Republic of Iran, Foreign policy shift, The first and second decade of the Islamic revolution.

INTRODUCTION

In the context of the dominant discourse in the first decade of the Islamic Revolution, some changes in economic and political structures had been seen, regarding the domestic and external challenges that were created for idealism (Iraq war against Iran, the death of Imam (RA), revision of the constitution, the isolation of Soviet union, etc.) and because of this discourse did not have ability to empower itself, its theoretical renewal and its consolidation, the country witnessed the transformation of the discourse of first decade of the revolution and the emergence of pragmatic discourse in second decade in which adjustment in domestic policy and detente in foreign policy were adopted. But it should be noted that in addition to internal factors that played an important role in the changes after the revolution, the structure of the international system had a great impact on these changes. In fact, the adoption of Resolution 598, the end of the Iran-Iraq war and the collapse of the Soviet Union and its impact on international relations were among the factors that in both domestic and international levels strongly influenced on policy-making process system, the way of people thinking and the way of the elite decision-making on major issues. In addition, the destruction of war and the ensuing financial and moral problems, destruction of production facilities and reduce the national capital, economic blockade, general economic turmoil and domestic political constraints were severely threatening the existence of the Islamic Republic, and also pursuing the policy of disregarding international arrangements during eight years of war, none of them could provide the revisionist International demands of Iran. Under the influence of these factors government gradually accepted the realities of the international system and internal situation of crisis with compulsion and regulating the internal situation and the country's economic reconstruction, economic reform (*i.e.* the transition from a war economy to a planned economy) and in the political arena, the normalization of relations were adopted by the government (Azghandi, 1387: 15).

1. THE IMPACT OF WAR ON THE FOREIGN POLICY IDEALISM DISCOURSE OF THE FIRST DECADE OF REVOLUTIONARY TO REALISM DISCOURSE OF SECOND DECADE

1.1. The Analysis of Foreign Policy Discourse During the War

Basically, the foreign policy of the Islamic Republic of Iran from 1359 to 1368 has two distinct features: the war conditions and the presence of the charismatic character of Imam Khomeini. These two factors together in highlighting the marginalization of the Islamists and other influential discourses had a great impact on the direction of foreign policy (Soltani, 1387: 147).

1.2. War and Interaction with the International System

Idealism discourse during the imposed war caused Iran created "built-in isolation" in its international relations (Aghaee, 1385: 2). So that in addition to the two poles of the world, the Soviet Union and the United States of America, major European countries as well as countries in the region, particularly members of Persian Gulf Cooperation Council besides reducing the level of their relations with the Islamic Republic of Iran sought to harness it. In the advent of Iraq attack to Iran in violation of its international borders, this was an opportunity for US to put Iran under pressure and tried to inhibit its revolutionary tendencies. Satisfaction of big powers including the US and the Soviet Union of Iraq invasion to Iran in September 1359 was clear in the declarations and requests of the United Nations from Iran and Iraq for exercising restraint and lack of Iraq conviction by the Security Council was evident. And European countries including Britain and France did not consider the ideals of the Islamic Revolution in line with for the world benefits of West industry and in relative harmony with the US joined to economic embargo of Iran and also during the war with Iraq practically tried to prevent Iraq's failure byequipping it with French Super-standard aircraft, French missiles, and German chemical weapons etc., And to neutralize the effects of the Islamic Revolution in area with isolation and harassment (Heidari, 1381: 40).

Soviet Union was pleased of the Islamic Revolution and the loss of US influence in a neighboring country but regarding the new political system of Iran's Islamic ideological and its hostility to the Marxist ideology and by sovereignty of neither East nor West slogan in foreign policy, the Soviets actually joined the ranks of countries opposing the Islamic revolution and due to the occurrence of some of the changes their relations strained more than ever. The suppression of the Tudeh Party of Iran, which in the past were known as agents of Soviet influence in Iran and more importantly Iran opposition against the Soviet invasion to Afghanistan and supporting the Afghan Mujahideen against the Soviet occupying forces and the ruling Communist regime in Afghanistan were the factors that raised Moscow's anger towards Islamic Iran. As a result, during the war, the Soviet Union was the main arms supplier to Iraq. Also, at the end of the war, by giving Scud missiles to Iraq played a prominent role in weakening Iran's economic and military power (Heidari, 1381: 40).

1.3. War and Iran's Interaction with the United Nations and the Security Council

Distrust and cynicism of Islamic Republic of Iran toward international organizations, especially the UN and its Security Council is considered one of the important features of wartime in foreign policy. Although the Islamic Republic of Iran based on its anti- domination approach considered International organizations as a tool of great power that legitimizing the status quo in favor of great powers. But the start of the war and the UN biased stance in favor of the aggressor during the war was the most important factor in the rejection of international organizations by the Islamic Republic of Iran. Virtually Islamic Republic of Iran boycottedthe UN Security Council as the sole source of international recognition and international peace and security.

1.4. The War-Torn Economy and the Issue of Country's Reconstruction after the War

With the onset of war and damaging oil installations and refineries in the industrial centers of the south and southwest of the country, and despite the high price of oil in world markets, Iran's oil revenues had declined due to lower exports. Economic sanctions from the West and blocking foreign exchange reserves were major reasons for the stagnation that has lasted 60 years. The country's economic problems affected different sectors and industrial activities due to their specific issues such as shortages of raw materials and imported raw materials and their high price in global markets, shortages and lack of access to machinery components and spare parts requirements, financial difficulties and a shortage of skilled manpower declined (Dejpasand, 1389: 95).

But at the end of the war (1367-1365) by Iraq escalation attack on economic centers, the expansion and escalation of oil tankers wars and the presence of armada powers of the East and the West, oil prices and oil revenues declined sharply. In this situation due to the escalation of restrictions on imports of capital and intermediate goods and raw materials, the cost of war and production costs had risen sharply. Therefore, government by increasing revenue and reducing costs eventually faced a budget deficit. In this period, economy of Iran had a great depression. Thus, in the wake of growing pressure from the political economy of war, the activity of various economic sectors was reduced and this trend continued until the end of the war. "(Dejpasand, 1389: 97).

2. DEMISE OF IMAM KHOMEINI (RA) AND REVISION OF THE CONSTITUTION AND ITS IMPACT ON THE FOREIGN POLICY DISCOURSE

2.1. Demise of Imam Khomeini (RA) and Its Impact on the Foreign Policy Discourse Changes

Iran's foreign policy which influenced by the strong leadership of Imam Khomeini took on ideological and idealistic dimension.

The changes in the second decade indicates that the demise of Imam Khomeini, and election of Ayatollah Khamenei in 1368 as his successor and the changes that occurred in the constitution the idealistic view of revolution was decreased in favor of pragmatic and realistic view. In addition to the leadership of Ayatollah Khamenei, the fifth presidential election was held in 1368. And in this election, Mr. Hashemi Rafsanjani became president with 5/94 percent of the vote and he selected his cabinet members also from political moderate faces and mostly technocratic and executive persons in order to fulfill his promise to rebuild the war destruction (Fawzi, 1387: 236).

2.2. The Revision of the Constitution and Its Impact on the Change in Foreign Policy Discourse

Another change in the late 60s that affected on the foreign policy of Islamic Republic of Iran from revolutionary idealism to pragmatic realism was the revision of the constitution in 1368. The chapter on foreign policy and the general principles relating to this policy into the constitution of 1358 can be considered a sort of manifesto of the ideals of the Islamic Revolution in dealing with the international system. The principles on which international relations and revisionism are emphasized from the Iranian nascent revolutionary; however, in its revised version remained unchanged, but institutional changes in the power structure of the leading and the Presidential bodies that occurred in revised constitution, the situations were provided to take practical and realistic views from principles. The new leaders of the Islamic Revolution of Iran, on the one hand, given the authority gained according to the modified constitution, and on the other hand, according to internal and external conditions and changes the new interpretations and model were adopted in accordance with the terms of the second decade of the revolution to meet the aspirations of their system in which these interpretations had fewer conflicts with existing structures in the international system and sought advancement of the goals of the revolution in this context.

3. THE IMPACT OF HASHEMI RAFSANJANI'S TECHNOCRAT'S GOVERNMENT IN FOREIGN POLICY DISCOURSE CHANGES FROM FIRST DECADE IDEALISM TO PRAGMATISM OF THE SECOND DECADE OF REVOLUTION

The construction period of the Islamic Republic of Iran (1368-1376) is an important period in the history of the Islamic Republic. At this historical period, foreign policy officials of Islamic Republic of Iran have adopted a pragmatic approach to constructive engagement with the outside world while adhering to the principles of Islamic fundamentalism. This was leading to the era of détente and by announcing détente was tried to adopt objectives in foreign policy, while meeting domestic demands, the foreign policy goals became consistent with existing international environment and one of the most important variables that had a significant impact on the adoption of pragmatism in foreign policy of the Iranian revolutionary regime in the second decade of the revolution was the emergence of Hashemi Rafsanjani's government and his technocratic brokers.

3.1. The Discourse of Hashemi State on Foreign Policy

The understanding of the political elites from world politics in the eight-year presidency of Hashemi Rafsanjani was more geopolitical than ideological. Therefore, great efforts with the flexibility and interest orientations were made to remove the political isolation of Iran. And a powerful Islamic Iran was held that can attract the attention of the international system (Ramezani, 1387: 74). The following principles can be named as the characteristics of this discourse:

1. Priority in relations between the states than relations between nations;
2. Conservatism and instrumental rationality in foreign policy;
3. Realism and paying attention to the mandate power and specifically to economic power;
4. Priority of vital national interests;
5. Accepting the primacy of the Islamic interests, ideological and national interests;
6. Inauthenticity of the status quo and deployed international order and accepting it as the secondary principle and expediency;
7. Consolidation of internal revolution and issuing it through economic patterning;
8. Being counter-arrogance by protesting on their intervention and developmental policy; and
9. Refuting interference in other countries' internal affairs (Dehghan Firoozabadi, 1384: 132-131).

It should be noted that during the construction period, reconstruction and economic development priorities is the subject that preoccupied the most senior officials of the Islamic Republic's mind. Hence, it was natural that in this regard, policies to realism were adopted in foreign policy of Iran because the reconstruction and economic development in an area that was considered by the macro policy-makers of the Islamic Republic should take place by making trust in the domestic, regional and international levels, the trust had vanished mostly due to revolutionary rhetoric and harsh slogans (and of course natural) at the beginning of the revolution. But Iran by using its geopolitical position in the world and enjoying it realized its position in the Middle East.

4. THE IMPACT OF INTERNATIONAL ECONOMIC AND POLITICAL DEVELOPMENTS ON THE FOREIGN POLICY DISCOURSE OF REVOLUTIONARY IDEALISM OF FIRST DECADE TO PRAGMATISM OF THE SECOND DECADE

4.1. The Collapse of the Bipolar System and End of the Cold War

The Islamic Republic of Iran with emphasis on core utility extensively tried to achieve their design principles in a bipolar system, regardless of the structure of the international system. But with the collapse of this regime, Iranian foreign policy has entered a new phase. Therefore, by changing the structure of the international system, desires of Islamic Republic of Iran was changed realistically. The priority of economic development that was crucial priority for national security in the aftermath of the war requires détente and expanding relations with different countries and in particular stabilizing the environment and security of Iran. This was the priority of Hashemi's discourse on foreign policy. To achieve this goal, détente and trust-building with neighboring countries and the region as well as with the less palatable countries was among the foreign policy priorities of Hashemi and thus, Iran entered a new phase of relations with neighbors and regional countries. And also relations with Europe and Asia were expanded so that these countries have participated in many economic activities. On the other hand, the cooperation with the Muslim world was expanded, so that Iran was chosen as the host of the summit of the Islamic Conference. Regarding regional cooperation, by the innovation of Islamic Republic of Iran Economic Cooperation Organization (ECO) was spread and during the summit in Tehran, its members increased from three to ten countries. Another indicator of the Hashemite' state, the active and constructive participation in regional developments can be mentioned. In this era, he has played a constructive role as a mediator in the Karabakh conflict and civil war in Tajikistan (Preacher, 1388: 283-281).

The collapse of the Soviet Union and the subsequent independence of the Soviet republics led Iran to new political geography of the area. Iran was the neighbor of just one country in the north and northwest borders (the Soviet Union) after collapsing Soviet Union and end of the Cold War, Iran became neighbor with central Asian republics and the Caucasus. After that changes in the international behavior of the United States about Iran happened that after Iran cutting ties due to Islamic revolution and the withdrawal of "CENTO alliance" and the dissolution of the alliance (NATO as the eastern branch), United States of America on the one hand sought to isolate Iran by embarking a strategy of dual containment that Iraq imposed war on Iran is one of the objectives of the strategy in which weakening economic and military fundamentals of the two opposed countries to US in the region for 8 years (Ezzati, 1380: 312). On the other hand, divergence tendency of former Soviet republics from Moscow's sphere of influence caused the opening of foothold of West, especially US and NATO in which influenced these republics by the promise of improving economic and social conditions in their areas. With this process, the United States and NATO allies, have expanded their influence in new republics and together with their Muslim ally in the region (Turkey) increased their influence in northern Iran, particularly in Caucasus and reduce Iran's presence and influence in the political- economic equation of these Republics. This issue demands high diplomatic activity to undo security threats of America and its regional allies by the Islamic Republic of Iran.

Along with the collapse of the bipolar system, the Persian Gulf War (1991) waited for an opportunity that Iran redefines its national security and represents new approach of foreign policy of the administration and shows its determination to show the change in the face of the international system. The new president pursued his work by avoiding enemy making, refusing to give an opportunity to the Iranian oppositions, détente, and expanding relations of Islamic Republic with other political units in the region and the world with the development of relations with European countries, the Soviet Union and Persian Gulf countries, the Middle East and northern and western neighbors of Iran and also reducing areas of divergence with US foreign policy.

As Ruhollah Ramazani said, "Iran's experience during the first decade of the revolution led to the new ideas that could be shown Iran how to deal with the new world without sacrificing Islamic ideals " (Ramezani, 1387, 74). In fact, the new foreign policy of the Iranian revolution principles was flexible and the trend toward governments more increased, and orientation of the external behavior of Iran-oriented was established on the basis of pragmatism. In the new framework, "the principles of peaceful coexistence and cooperative policy based on trust" was regarded as a priority. On the whole, relations between Iran and Europe, Soviet Union, China, Japan and countries in the region expanded (Ardestani, 1393: 48).

4.2. The Impact of Economic Developments on the International System

The programs and neoliberal policies that are called "structural adjustment" policies rooted in the "Washington Consensus" were taken seriously under the same name by Hashemi Rafsanjani government to rebuild the destruction caused by the war. A year after the war between Iran and Iraq, "reconstruction" time had come. The government needed budget and the International Monetary Fund and the World Bank announced their readiness to meet these needs, but with a precondition: implementing policies of "adjustment." In fact, Hashemi Rafsanjani technocratic cabinet realistically concluded: The political and economic reconstruction of the country depends on creating a secure environment and to achieve this important goal, political detente and as Professor Alireza Azghandi said, abstaining from inciting others in order to open the World Economic Capital in Iran should be considered the first priority.

CONCLUSION

The Islamic Revolution in February 1357, expanded the Islamist and religious tendencies and with a touch of idealism, broadened its revolutionary movements. Ideological and idealistic space from 1357 to 1367 that was exacerbated by the outbreak of the war is not covert to anyone. In the second decade of the changes that occurred in the realities of environmental and social values basket, the kind of challenges facing the system was changed. Several developments in the domestic and international levels led to the transition to the second period (pragmatism). Unprecedented coincidence of dramatic changes in the power structure inside and outside of Iran (internal structure and the structure of the international system) has gradually changed the policy of revolutionary Iran. Inside of Iran, the end of the Iran-Iraq war, Imam Khomeini's death on June 68, and the emergence role of Ayatollah Khamenei as a leader, amending the constitution and increasing executive powers, and outside of Iran, the Persian Gulf War of 1991, the end of the Cold War and the collapse of the Soviet Union, Slowly but firmly changed the teachings and practices of Iran in the field of foreign policy. Structural changes in the international system that was started from détente and the subsequently, end of the Cold War and the collapse of the Soviet Union and finally led to the end of the bipolar system and the international system was in transition, and collapsing bipolar system imposed the unexpected local and environmental conditions on Iran. The factors are mentioned above as sources of internal and external environmental changes, had its dramatic effects on both the value construction and the realities of environmental. The end of the Iran-Iraq war, the demise of the founder of the Islamic Revolution, the end of the Cold War and the collapse of the Soviet Union were on top of these changes.

In Iran's foreign policy orientation, by taking power by the revolutionary forces and creating the civil and political cohesion, especially after the end of the war, the importance of accuracy and computing in domestic and foreign politics was felt more than ever which began with the launch of the government of Mr

Hashemi Rafsanjani. He began to underpin coherent and purposeful foreign policy carefully and with knowledge of country priorities and constraints with regard to domestic, regional and international conditions. And in this process, he insisted on the principle of détente especially at the regional level. Regarding pragmatism of Hashemi Rafsanjani along adherence to the principles of the revolution for the establishment of a powerful Iran to attract attention of the international system, a major effort was done by him with the flexibility to come out Islamic Republic from political isolation that imposed in eight years of war. To this end, Hashemi in order to be closer to West and use their support began critical dialogue with European countries. And to reduce the risks of dual containment policy of America, improved trade relations with America and signed the lucrative contracts with US companies so that in practice until 1371, America was fifth exporter of goods to the Iranian government and American oil companies became the main buyers of crude oil. Akbar Hashemi Rafsanjani also emphasized the preservation of Amalaqra to avoid further confrontation with the Islamic Republic of Arabic-Islamic countries refused to continue to express the slogan of "spreading revolution". Construction elites asserted that "if the Islamic Republic succeeded with the reconstruction and economic modernization to achieve the necessary economic growth and development... it will encourage Muslims to follow and emulate it." Therefore, the revolution lost the physical and military content and was defined as synonymous with the pattern of offering economic development of the Islamic Republic to other countries, mainly Muslim countries.

REFERENCES

Aghaee, Sayed Dawood (1385). "The foreign policy of the Islamic Republic of Iran during the eight-year war (by looking at the position of the European Community in this policy)". *Journal of Law and Political Science*, 73.

Ehteshami, Anushiravan (1378). Iranian Politics during Construction, Tehran, Islamic Revolution Documents Center.

Ardestani, H. (1382). The Iran-Iraq war chronology, The Book Fifty-Second World Scrambling to Stop the War, Tehran: Centre for War Studies.

Azghandi, A.R. (1378). "Détente in Foreign Policy of the Islamic Republic of Iran (781, 367)". *Foreign Policy Journal*, XIII(4).

Dejpasand, F. and Hamidreza, Raoofi (1378). The Iranian economy during the war, Tehran: Centre for War Studies.

Dehghani Firoozabadi, S.J. and Firooze, Radfar (1389). Patterns of revolution in foreign policy of the Islamic Republic of Iran, Tehran: University of Imam Sadeq (AS).

Ramezani, R. (1387). Analytical framework for the foreign policy of the Islamic Republic of Iran, Tehran: Ney publication.

Soltani, Seyed Ali Asghar (1383). "Discourse theory as a theory and method". *Journal of Political Science*, 28(1383).

Ezzati (1380). The glory of god geopolitics twenty-first century, Tehran: Samat Publication.

Fawzi, Y. (1387). Political and social developments in Iran after the Islamic Revolution, 1380-1357, Volume II, Tehran: Orooj publication.

Vaezi, Mahmoud (1388). Mediation in Central Asia and the Caucasus, Islamic Republic of Iran, Tehran: Publications Center of the Ministry of Foreign Affairs.

7

From Soviet Union to Russia: Can Democracy Gain Ground?

TAMANNA KHOSLA[1]*

ABSTRACT

The article aims to look at the movement from autocratic Soviet Union to semi democratic Russia under Putin. The current Russian society is in crisis. Putin's innovations coincide with a spate of revisionist thinking about democratization in the contemporary world. Some say that autocracies are being replaced, as often as not, by hybrid regimes entwining democratic with authoritarian principles. Others go further, asserting that Russia and a series of other countries are best thought of as "competitive-authoritarian" systems, in which the authoritarian element has the upper hand. So this is what the article aims to focus on.

***Key words*:** Democracy, Liberal democracy, Managerial democracy, Federalism, Institutionalism.

[1] Department of Political Science, Delhi College of Arts and Commerce, Delhi University

**Corresponding E-mail*: tamannakhosla@gmail.com

I. INTRODUCTION: ONSET OF LIBERAL DEMOCRACY IN RUSSIA

The current Russian society is in crisis. Putin's innovations coincide with a spate of revisionist thinking about democratization in the contemporary world. Some say that autocracies are being replaced, as often as not, by hybrid regimes entwining democratic with authoritarian principles. Others go further, asserting that Russia and a series of other countries are best thought of as "competitive-authoritarian" systems, in which the authoritarian element has the upper hand[1].

But a century ago, Russia was a hotbed not only of radical socialism but also liberalism. From 1905 to 1917 the Constitutional Democrats were a significant political force and in 1906 Finland, then part of the Russian Empire, became the first part of Europe to extend suffrage to women. But the fact also needs to be understood that this phase of democracy disappeared soon after establishment of communist Soviet Russia.

This phase of Soviet Russia was replaced by a more democratic phase of Russian federation. Although some might disagree, it is clear that some form of democracy emerged in Russia after the collapse of Soviet communism in 1991. While not displaying the thick structures and norms typical of a mature "liberal democracy," the Russian regime that put down roots under Boris Yeltsin in the 1990s has many of the features of an "electoral democracy"[2].

The Russian state and Russian society displayed features of democratic development[3]. Elections took place under a set of rules recognized by all. The results of these elections were not entirely certain beforehand, and no authority intervened after Election Day to reverse the outcome of the voting. The playing field for competitors in elections was never equal and has steadily become less so. Nonetheless, the rulers of Russia were selected in competitive elections. The regime that emerged in the 1990s was qualitatively different from the communist and tsarist dictatorships.

The interceding years obviously took a different turn but recent changes present the biggest opportunity since 1917 for liberalism to gain a hold in Russia. The nature of recent protests against Vladimir Putin's less than democratic accession to the Presidency once again shows the emergence of a politically astute and concerned middle class. Putin will have to introduce reforms to tackle corruption and improve democracy if he is to maintain his grip on power.

II RUSSIA'S MANAGED DEMOCRCY VERSUS AMERICAN DEMOCRACY

But the fact is that Russia faces a lot of challenges as far as setting up of a liberal agenda. Russia has to face America in its collective psyche. If America did not exist, Russia would have to invent it. It could be described as dread of the other. No country looms as large in the Russian Psyche as America in today's Russia. Anti-Americanism has long been a staple of Vladimir Putin, but it has undergone an important shift. Now it neither pretends nor aspires to be like west. Instead it wants to take off from American influence.

The Russians have shut of all cooperation that uses American money including on health care, civil society, trafficking, drugs and dismantling of unconventional weapons. Some Russian deputies have even suggested fining of cinemas which show too many foreign movies.

Further for instance Kremlin has banned American couples from adopting Russian children. Putins second response was a law introduced prohibiting Russian officials from holding foreign banks because such a thing pose a threat to national security.

Yet it has not boosted Putin's popularity in any way or restored trust in his term as the president of Russia. Infact number of Russians viewing America as a friend rather than foe has increased over the years. This might be due to growing mistrust of Kremlin. That is what made soviet propaganda ineffective 30 years back.

Russian society also seems to have limited interest in growing political role of the church.

Russia's Institutional Structure

Especially after the enactment of Yeltsin's super-presidential constitution in 1993, mass-based interest groups were consigned to the fringes, pluralist interest intermediation became feeble, individual liberties began to be abridged by arbitrary practices, and institutions that could have helped to redress the imbalance-parliament, the party system, the judiciary-lost strength and independence.

According to Tom Bjorkman

- Power remains concentrated in the executive branch and centered on informal networks and personal connections.
- Legislative and judicial institutions remain fragile.
- Protections for civil liberties are weak, and state harassment of independent journalists and civic activists is on the rise[4].
- Official corruption remains pervasive and movement toward a rule of law glacial.

There is currently no legal recognition of same-sex couples in Russia, and same-sex marriages are not allowed. Public support for gay marriages is at 14% as of 2005. Further same sex couple are not allowed to adopt.

Kremlin has imposed its traditionalist agenda on Russian society by prosecuting Pussy Riot, the punk singer who performed obscenely on the altar of Russia's main cathedral, by banning the promotion of homosexuality.

Soviet Union saw lot of repression of freedom of expression and was a totalitarian system. Reagan said, "Let us be aware that while they preach the supremacy of the state, declare its omnipotence over individual man, predict its eventual domination of all peoples of the Earth, they are the focus of evil in the modern world,".

Since Vladimir Putin became president at the beginning of 2000, democratic institutions have eroded. When Yeltsin appointed Putin prime minister in the fall of 1999, the regime's uncertain and unconsolidated nature lowered the barriers for institutional change. Putin soon put his imprint not only on policy but on institutions. He has not amended or radically violated the 1993 constitution, and he has not upended the institutional configuration of Yeltsin's regime. Nor does he seem to have any coherent plan for doing so. He has, however, initiated or tolerated a series of discrete changes that have diminished the democratic legacy of the reform years.

Russian Democracy and Federalism

Putin has assembled super-majorities in the Duma-majorities capable of overriding vetoes of bills handed down by the Federation Council, the upper house of parliament. As a result, he has been able to transform the organization of the upper house and therefore the federal system. To everyone's surprise, Putin made reform of the Federation Council one of his top political goals in his first months in office. Two weeks after he was sworn into office, Putin proposed a new recipe for the upper house that replaced the regional leaders with persons designated by them under an intricate formula. The members of the Federation Council resisted tenaciously, knowing they would lose their apartments and offices in Moscow, their parliamentary immunity, and much of their clout with the federal government. After a heated battle, in which the Duma said it would override a Federation Council veto and the Kremlin allegedly threatened governors with criminal investigations if they did not support Putin's plan, the law was adopted in July 2000[5].

Putin's clipping of the governors' wings was extended to their home turf by a decree enacted on May 13, 2000. The decree established seven super-regions ("federal districts"), accountable to Moscow, and super-imposed them on the eighty-nine units of the federation. Each super-region was to be headed by a plenipotentiary appointed by the president and sitting on his Security Council. Five of the seven envoys named in 2000 were from the Federal Security Service (FSB), the army, or the police. Their writ extends to every federal agency in the regions other than the military forces, and thus they have access to officials in the politically most sensitive and influential agencies, such as the treasury, the tax inspectorate, the procuracy, the FSB, and the regular police. Their mission is to oversee the activities of the bureaucracy and report to the president's office on any regional noncompliance with the constitution or the law.

Three other changes accompanied the super-regions. First, a law passed in July 2000 authorizes the president to suspend elected governors accused of wrongdoing by the procurator-general's office. Inasmuch as criminal proceedings can drag on indefinitely (especially if it suits the president), the law is tantamount to a presidential right to fire governors. Putin has used the power only once, and indirectly at that (when he orchestrated the ouster of Governor Evgenii Nazdratenko of Primorsky Krai in 2001), but the mere threat of it has had a chilling effect on gubernatorial initiative. Putin can also dismiss any regional legislature that passes laws contravening federal laws or the constitution. Second, Putin's government has stopped signing the bilateral agreements with the provinces that were one of Yeltsin's favorite instruments for winning their acquiescence. As of 2003, the division of labor among the national and subnational governments is to be governed by an omnibus law that in principle is to be applied uniformly across Russia. Third, Moscow has pushed through a more centralized allotment of tax receipts. As of 1999, roughly 45 percent of the revenues collected in the regions were supposed to be transferred to the central government, but the amount that reached it was often smaller. Under a law signed by Putin in 2000, about 55 percent is to go to Moscow and 45 percent to the regions, and the balance is to be reviewed regularly. Regions like Bashkortostan, which for years paid almost no federal taxes by a virtue of bilateral agreement, are once again contributing to the federal budget.

But as we have seen earlier in the article, Russian people are now struggling to bring about more freedom, the middle class world over is keen on the need for democracy and against authoritarian kind of set up Russia like several other countries has been moving towards the need for liberalism and democracy.

III PUTINS REPRESSIVE RUSSIA

However under Vladimir Putins irony is that the Kremlin's anti Americanism reveals not its independence but its reliance on America as an enemy. The real casualty may be Russia itself. It is the people who will suffer in Putin's Russia. Liberalism and democracy are the basic need of present nation states. The US economist Richard W. Rahn called Putinism "a Russian nationalistic authoritarian form of government that pretends to be a free market democracy", which "owes more of its lineage to fascism than communism;" noting that "Putinism depended on the Russian economy growing rapidly enough that most people had rising standards of living and, in exchange, were willing to put up with the existing soft repression", he predicted that "as Russia's economic fortunes changed, Putinism was likely to become more repressive. Russian historian Andranik Migranyan saw the Putin regime as restoring what he believed were the natural functions of a government after period of the 1990s, when Russia was allegedly ruled by oligopolies expressing only their narrow interests. He said, "If democracy is the rule by a majority and the protection of the rights and opportunities of a minority, the current political regime can be described as democratic, at least formally.

Russian politician Boris Nemtsov and commentator Kara-Murza define Putinism in Russia as a one party system, censorship, a puppet parliament, ending of an independent judiciary, firm centralization of power and finances, and hypertrophied role of special services and bureaucracy, in particular in relation to business.

Russia's nascent middle class showed few signs of political activism under the regime, as Masha Lipman reported as with the majority overall, those in the middle-income group have accepted the paternalism of Vladimir Putin's government and remained apolitical and apathetic. The lack of strong opposition parties and the central state's ability to intervene in local elections underscore the weakness of the checks on the Kremlin's power.

Russian Party System

Russia's party system does not perform the role that party systems play in working democracies. Most of the country's parties lack a distinct identity or a stable following. They have little effect on the elections that count, the ones in which the president and the regional administrative heads are chosen. Russian electoral law assigns political parties a pivotal role in parliamentary elections, but nonpartisans and weak party organizations continue to play a critical role. Finally, there is little internal cohesion within the parties that remainakened with time.

Whatever comes of these partisan intrigues and squabbles, there are two other changes underway that must be watched for their long-term effects. The first stems from the interest of the Russian leadership in revamping the rules for party formation and State Duma elections. Addressing Unity's convention in February 2000, Putin spoke in favor of a "workable" party system made up of "two, three, or four parties"[5]. Streamlining was the main aim of a new law on parties passed in 2001, which stiffened the requirements for registration and stipulated that electoral blocs would now have to include one political party. In 1999, Unity called for an end to proportional representation and for all deputies to be elected in districts. Its motivations were not altruistic. Unity's poor showing in the districts in 1999 notwithstanding, its founders calculated that a party of power would do better in a district-based system, especially if it could polarize the district races and then prevail in the runoff. Unity and its Duma allies have so far failed to institute such a change, but in 2002, they raised the threshold for the party list from 5 to 7 percent, effective in 2007 (they originally proposed 12.5 percent), which will decrease the number of parties that get into parliament. Putin's brain trust hopes eventually to push all parties other than Unified Russia and the KPRF to the sidelines[6]. If the communists and Unified Russia were to cooperate in getting rid of proportional representation altogether, Russia's proto-multiparty system might easily become a hegemonic party system dominated by Unified Russia[7].

The second and more alarming trend is toward arbitrary interference by the central authorities in regional elections, usually with the connivance of local politicos, electoral commissions, and courts. The tone was set in November 2000, when Kremlin officials pressured a judge to remove the incumbent, Aleksandr Rutskoi.

Russia and International Relations

Wars are always brutal, and Chechnya is no exception, but the violence of the guerrillas and the terrorists linked to them does not exonerate Russia's routinely inhumane actions. Human Rights Watch has documented atrocities that include summary shootings, the torching of villages, the rape of Chechen women, and the mistreatment of prisoners of war. Experts reckon that the fighting has displaced 400,000 refugees[8]. Moscow has no strategy for either withdrawal or a negotiated settlement. The March 2003 referendum on Chechnya's status, in which more than 90 percent of its citizens supposedly endorsed all three of Moscow's questions, was a farce, emphasizing yet again the lack of a serious plan to end the bloodshed. To stanch the flow of information about human rights violations, Russia has expelled the observer mission of the Organization for Security and Cooperation in Europe from the republic

In December 2007, the Russian sociologist Igor Eidman (VCIOM) categorized the Putin regime as "the power of bureaucratic oligarchy" which had "the traits of extreme right-wing dictatorship — the dominance of state-monopoly capital in the economy, silovoki structures in governance, clericalism and statism in ideology"

In August 2008, The Economist wrote about the virtual demise of both Russian and Soviet intelligentsia in post-Soviet Russia and noted: Putinism was made strong by the absence of resistance from the part of society that was meant to provide intellectual opposition.

In early February 2009, Aleksander Auzan, an economist and board member at a research institute set up by Dmitry Medvedev, said that in the Putin system, "there is not a relationship between the authorities and the people through Parliament or through nonprofit organizations or other structures. The relationship to the people is basically through television. And under the conditions of the crisis, that can no longer work. In May 2000, The Guardian wrote: "When a band of former Soviet dissidents declared in February that Putinism was nothing short of modernised Stalinism, they were widely dismissed as hysterical prophets of doom. 'Authoritarianism is growing harsher, society is being militarised, the military budget is increasing,' they warned, n 2000, Russia's political analyst Andrei Piontkovsky called Putinism "the highest and culminating stage of bandit capitalism in Russia". He said: "Russia is not corrupt. Corruption is what happens in all countries when businessmen offer officials large bribes for favors. Today's Russia is unique. The businessmen, the politicians, and the bureaucrats are the same people. They have privatized the country's wealth and taken control of its financial flows. The term Mafia state has been used by some Western media to describe the political system in Russia under Vladimir Putin's rule. The term came to prominence following the United States diplomatic cables leak, which revealed that US diplomats viewed Putin's Russia as a "a corrupt, autocratic kleptocracy centred on the leadership of Vladimir Putin, in which officials, oligarchs and organised crime are bound together to create a 'virtual mafia state'.

IV RUSSIAS AUTHORITARIAN DEMOCRACY

Democracy is thus not held much ground after demise of Soviet Union. Russian democracy is not just in crisis; politically speaking it has ceased to exist. It is not represented in the parliament, it has disappeared as a focus of public debates, even among intellectuals, and its claims to be a credible and politically attractive ideology now seem vain if not preposterous. The term "Russian democracy" is used as an umbrella concept embracing the political practices and agencies, both of the neoliberal and social liberal types, which identified the Russian "exit from Communism" with the establishment of the rule of law, political and ideological pluralism, the market economy and "openness to the West", if not its imitation. Neither the repressive nature of the present regime nor the innate hostility of the Russian "cultural tradition" towards liberalism and democracy can explain this calamity. These are pseudo-explanations that serve Russian liberals as pretexts for their own self-exculpation. If liberalism is to be reborn in Russia, one must understand the political causes of its demise. Liberalism and democracy failed as an ideology in Russia in the wake of communism's collapse. Now Russian liberals must free themselves from the burden of the Boris Yeltsin legacy – its unabashed neoliberalism – and confront the type of capitalism expressed by the present Russian regime's "authoritarian capitalism." The mass anti-communist movement at the end of Russia's perestroika era was liberal in spirit. Liberty and human rights, equality and justice, non-violence and the rejection of economic and political dirigisme made up the "nodal points" of its alternative to the status quo. Unfortunately, self-proclaimed "democrats" opted for sequencing reforms according to a formula of market first, democracy next. Suffice to say that, at least in the specific circumstances of Russia, such sequencing resulted in a distorted and socially harmful free market presided over by a bunch of warring oligarchs. Instead of promoting a transition from Communism to the "blessed plateau" of democratic capitalism, it allowed the undemocratic misdeeds of Yeltsin's regime and the appalling depravity of the huge portions of the population of Russia. But instead of showing outrage, many liberals considered this as a reasonable price that Russia had to pay for being pulled out from communism. Liberals continued to trumpet their values of human rights and private property. Up to the end of the 1990s, the regime of authoritarian capitalism had not been consolidated. The future autocrats still needed the Russian liberal intelligentsia as one of their props. So when Vladimir Putin took over as Russia's President he was careful to preserve the semblance of the liberals' participation in politics, even co-opting certain of them as "advisors", "experts" and functionaries of the regime. Those who were determined to put their liberal beliefs into practice were later ejected from their positions and the rest were assimilated into the rising and solidifying bureaucracy of authoritarian capitalism. The liberals' "moment of truth" arrived with the new century, when the regime realised that it could henceforth perpetuate itself without recourse to the liberal intelligentsia. The liberals were found politically redundant and the regime abandoned rather than persecuted them. On their own, the liberals could not survive politically. This is what predetermined the electoral failures in 2003 of parties like Yabloko and the Union of the Rightist Forces.

It could charitably be said that the Russian liberal intelligentsia suffered from its own excessive idealism, and that it's somewhat naïve dedication to ideals lacked practical executioners. The same liberals today castigate the regime, and with good reason. The absence of an independent judiciary, severe limitations of the freedom of the mass media, rampant corruption in all branches of bureaucracy and the systematic harassment of nearly all opposition are genuine ills. It is one thing, though, to articulate all these grievances and quite another to set out an attractive and politically mobilising ideology. Russia's liberals have to send forth a message that resonates with the broader public. The resonance can't just be some sort of rehearsal of the "superstitions" of the people; it means coming up with a compelling alternative.

A dialogue between liberals in Russia and the West can therefore only be beneficial, not just for each other's political systems but ultimately for each other's economies. For Russian liberalism to finally succeed, it will a need a leader who is different from the current ones. Preferably, this person should not come from the Moscow or St. Petersburg intelligentsia, or/and not be perceived, by ordinary Russians, as an aloof bonehead with little empathy for the worries and needs of ordinary Russians, outside the metropoles. Ideally, this new leader would have an acute understanding of the need for coalition building and compromise finding. He/she should be person who actually wants to reach, and work in, a high position in the Russian executive – rather than impressively perform in scholarly debates or at international symposia. Russian liberalism, in short, needs a real politician and not yet another intelligent, at its helm. Further for liberalism to succeed the need would be for new institutions to take place. Thus there hasn't been much difference from Soviet Union to Russia as far as setting up of democratic principles are concerned. Thus while new democratic parties have come up, Mr. Putins style of politics still continues. Russia thus need not ape west but have its own version of democracy and liberalism.

V CONCLUSION

Russia: A Managed Democracy

It is premature to pigeonhole Russia into any of these autocratic categories. The phrase "managed democracy" will do as a marker for the current condition of its polity. If it is too early to sign the death certificate for democracy, it is too late to ignore tokens of a backing away from the liberal and democratic ideals in which name the Soviet regime was overthrown. Having begun on Yeltsin's watch, the retreat has gathered momentum under Putin. Russia's present rulers are modernizers in the economic and socioeconomic sphere and pro-Western realists in foreign policy.

For those at the rudder, democracy is neither good nor evil. It is an existential product of larger forces that, like gravity, cannot be stopped, yet, with the appropriate engineering, can be harnessed to one's own purpose. Institutional change under Putin has reflected this odd blend of preserving formal democratic practices and at the same time weakening the actual democratic content of these political rules and norms to liberal democratic status by 2008.

The impact on the regime of Putin's rise to power suggests that the current political system has not consolidated. Russia's nascent democracy is on a negative trajectory, but the unconsolidated state of the regime gives some cause for hope. The regime has not become a total dictatorship. Whether Putin even wants to create such a regime is an open question. Whether he could is also uncertain. Although weak throughout the 1990s and weaker today than just two years ago, democratic rules and procedures are still embedded in the regime, and democratic norms permeate society[9]. Above all else, every major political actor in Russia today believes that elections are the only legitimate way to choose national leaders. No serious leader or political force in Russia today has articulated an alternative model to democracy. For the near future, Putin and his advisers seem likely to manage a version of democracy that limits real political competition and blocks the strengthening of alternative sources of political power. During new crises or after unforeseen events, "managed democracy" can become unmanageable, and pseudo democratic institutions may suddenly gain real democratic content. The experience of Slobodan Milosevic in the former Yugoslavia and Leonid Kuchma in Ukraine demonstrates how formal democratic rules can suddenly and surprisingly undermine the best plans for "managing democracy.

In Russia, though, the most likely outcome for the near future is neither more democracy nor more autocracy-neither liberal democracy nor dictatorship-but a stable regime somewhere in between. Putin has eroded democratic institutions and practices but has not destroyed them, nor has he articulated a plan for their further erosion Russian society seems content with the current quasi-democratic, quasi autocratic order. Russians value democracy but are too exhausted, from decades of turmoil, to fight for better democracy. Stability is the greater priority. Managed democracy could be around in Russia for a long time.

REFERENCES

[1] Colton Timothy J. and McFaul Michael (2003). Russian Democracy under Putin. *Problems of Post Communism (Journal)*, 50(4).
[2] Ibid.
[3] To look at the differences between electoral and liberal democracies, see Larry Diamond, Developing Democracy: Toward Consolidation (Baltimore: Johns Hopkins University Press, 1999)
[4] https://www.brookings.edu/research/russian-democracy-and-american-foreign-policy/
[5] ibid.
[6] RFE/RL Newsline (February 28, 2000)
[7] Pointing in a more positive direction is the 2002 federal law mandating proportional representation for 50 percent of the seats in local and regional legislatures. The law creates incentives for party building at the subnational level, where it has gone at a snail's pace for the past decade. See the statement by Aleksandr Veshniakov of the Central Electoral Commission (www.cikrf.ru/_1_en/doc_2_1/
[8] See, for instance, articles in the OSCE publication Russia/Chechnya: "Now Happiness Remains: Civilian Killings, Pillage, and Rape in Alkhan-Yurt," 12, no. 5 (April 2000): 1-33; "February 5: A Day of Slaughter in Novye Aldi," 12, no. 9 (June 2000): 1-43; "The 'Dirty War' in Chechnya: Forced Disappearances, Torture, and Summary Executions," 13, no. 1 (March 2001): 1-42; "Burying the Evidence: The Botched Investigation into a Mass Grave in Chechnya," 13, no. 3 (May 2001): 1-26. John Dunlop's Chechnya Weekly, published by the Jamestown Foundation, also provides full coverage of the war, including human rights violations. There is extensive discussion of the first and second wars in Matthew Evangelista, The Chechen Wars: Will Russia Go the Way of the Soviet Union? (Washington, DC: Brookings Institution Press, 2003).
[9] On the differences between "politically close authoritarian," or full-blown dictatorship, and "competitive authoritarian," see Diamond, "Thinking about Hybrid Regimes"; Levitsky and Way, "Rise of Competitive Authoritarianism."

8

Quest for Democratization in Morocco and Roles of the Monarchy

GHAZALI BELLO ABUBAKAR[1]*

ABSTRACT

Occurrence of the dual unforgettable incidents namely 'Cold War' between the two super powers, the United States and the former United Soviet Socialist Republic (USSR) and fall of the Berlin Wall, Moroccan authorities consolidated what could be seen as "fundamental background" of democratization process. With the help of modernity, Moroccan monarchy has been able to incrementally install a systematic equilibrium that could match the contemporarily modern democratic style. The authorities however, focus on political and civil organizations. The flexible nature of this nation coupled with absolute amenable behaviour to embrace democracy as a new style very much help in keeping kingship system on the stance at least for now and time to come. This has become clear during the popular political revolts of 2011 when Moroccans in large numbers demanded modifications and changes instead of toppling down the entire ancient system. Islam reached Morocco somewhere during the first century of the Hijra

[1] Faculty of Arts and Social Science, Department of Political Science, Sokoto State University, Sokoto, Nigeria.

Corresponding E-mail: alghazel@gmail.com

(migration), and since that time, the kingship remains the style of leadership in the country until today.

***Key words*:** Democratization process, Moroccan regime, reform, Hassan II era, Roles of King Muhammad VI.

INTRODUCTION

For the past several decades, Kingdom of Morocco has become one of the targeted realms of the world powers. Long ago, donor and pro-democracy nations have been emphasizing peace and political transition, human rights, and transparency in the country. Addition to that, the historical linkages and relationships that the Kingdom of Morocco maintains with the western world including the United States are tremendously serving an outstanding remark in transforming and preparing Morocco for the current political scenario (except for the issue of Western Sahara). It is very difficult for Morocco to suddenly switch-off her ancient style, which is in the place for more than 1300 years back to adopt a newly democratized style.

Perhaps, abolishing kingship style and putting in place democratic leadership could not be unsurpassed for Moroccan current political and economic situations. Therefore, the sluggish step-by-step mechanism seems quite proper in order to embrace full and stable democratic system in this country whose citizens are dominantly Muslims. Democracy can be good for people of countries such as Egypt, Libya, Tunisia or any "Third World" states if it can be applied step by step on incremental approach depending on the background of leadership on the ground and orientation of citizens of any given nation.

The Kingdom of Morocco is said to be one of the moderate Arab-Muslim states, likewise the Hashemite Kingdom of Jordan. However, in terms of transition to representative and liberal democracy, Morocco proves to be heavyweight since 1990s. So many factors contribute in achieving regular peaceful transitions including geographic proximity to the countries of south Europe, which has brought about many influences on Moroccan culture, tradition and language. Secondly, the country's old friendship and relation with the United States, the biggest producer of modern and liberal democracy, is another added value.

It is beyond doubt that these factors must have helped Morocco shaping her political ambitious future. Compared to the previous past, many improvements are witnessed in various walking of life; freedom of speech is wider, enlarging political participation, more chances for civil society groups, etc.

To sketch out roles played by Moroccan regime so to ensure consolidation of democratization process, this study looks at some key areas including nature of conducting elections, social issues like education, health, transportation, and other social amenities. Lack of these facilities could effectively undermine the ongoing process.

CONCEPTUAL CLARIFICATION

The word 'Democracy' that signifies absolute free will of peoples to elect who should govern their affairs is non-English origin neither a modern concept. Rather, it gets its fertile ground in the primordial time. Like many *'cracy'* ending words, such as aristo*cracy*, bureau*cracy* and so forth, 'democracy' is a product of Ancient Greece. For Greek lingua-franca of Indo-European language family (Hellenic language), *'Demos'* stands for 'peoples' or 'many', while *'kratos'* and/or *'cracy'*, in modern English letters, means, 'power' or 'rule'. Therefore, the modern definition of democracy is nothing but the rule of the people, by the people and for the people, where everyone has an equal share, alike as promoted by Abraham Lincoln.

The ideological term 'democracy' and freedom however, seem to have their genetic roots alongside beginning of human civilization. Meanwhile, partially, the principles of governance based on democracy became popular and universal norms only in the twentieth century. Paradoxically, more than one definition speculates to review the limit of democracy, albeit there could hardly be a sentence that rhetorically contains meanings of what democracy is all about. The word 'democracy' according to David Held came into English vernacular somewhere in the sixteenth century from the French *democratie*, while its origins were Greek. 'Democracy' means a form of government, in contradistinction to monarchies and aristocracies, of the people rule. Democracy entails a political community in which there is some form of political equality among the people. The history of the idea of democracy is complex and marked by conflicting conceptions. There are plenty scopes for disagreement (Held, 2006: 01).

Democracy is seen as a system in which, both rulers and ruled, govern, share and involve in general policy decision-making with equal power. Democracy has been also recognized and chiefly treated as the best form of government. In other words, the concept is just opposite of autocracy, monarchy, dictatorship, authoritarianism, absolutism, oligarchy, hierarchy tyranny or any kind of arbitrary ruling. Out of the above different forms of governments, no single form prolongs to serve the cause of the people directly. Therefore, the exponents of "democracy" got and are still getting popularity in advocating the suitability of the democratic form for the global setting of today simply because it seems to go side by side with good governance and humanitarian considerations. Prominent scholars, such as John Austin (1790-1859), A.V Dicey (1835-1922) and A.L Lowell (1856-1943) were some of the exponents of the democratic system of government.

THEORETICAL FRAMEWORK

Putatively, democracy appears to be the most accredited system that has developed an apparatus to balance between the two classes, rulers and ruled and claims to be a government of all as mentioned above. Since it is emerging as universal norm, good governance is always expected in its platform. R.M. Dworkin highlights that, democracy means government by the people.

Nevertheless, what does that means? Among political theories or in the dictionary, no explicit definition of democracy is settled. On the contrary, it is a matter of deep controversy of what democracy really means. Even though people disagree on which techniques of representation and which level: local, state, and national governments allocates power, and which other institutional arrangements provide the best available version of democracy, (Dworkin, 1999: 15).

As a form of government, numerous scholars defined democracy terms of sources of authority for government, purposes served by government, and for constituting government (Huntington, 1991). No doubt, many people believe that democracy should be the best system to administer people compared to the non-democratic regimes, which many, however, adduce to be incapable ideal form of leadership. Arguably, democracy is more qualified and qualitative configuration ever runs by more educative class with less aggressive and violent basis, and highly caring for the people, conscious to deliver up their duties based on equality, liberty and welfare. Yet the idea identifying democracy as government formed by the people and, for the people, as suggested by more than exponent, and if the statement is to upgrade greater participation of the entire citizens, it never review the limit of democracy.

To point out democracy as 'rule of the people' does not make things clear unless we know what or who constitutes the peoples. If 'by people' means we all the adults without any other qualification attached to it, we may not have the rule of the people, because all the people do not rule, and in fact, cannot rule. If 'by people', we mean those who participate in decision-making or administering or legislating, then such a system would be ruled by the few, and not of all the people. So considered, the rule of the majority would also not be democratic since it would exclude the few-minority. Despite the worldly remarkable recognition that democracy enjoys, throughout twentieth and twenty-first centuries, regardless the over-heating arguments on how democracy ought to be, still many questions arise on whether the available democratic countries in the world success or fail.

Over the past two decades or so, the study of democratization has become a branch and the most important area in the field of political science and other related disciplines. Democracy requires strong local government, multiparty system, equal participation and political rights of citizens, civil liberties and the multitude of non-governmental organizations. A stable democracy needs a certain level of both social and economic well-being, including widespread literacy, urbanization and high per capita incomes.

In the formal foundation of democracy, history shows that, apart from Ancient Greece, the society considered the pioneer of the ideological concept; different societies and cultures were being governed through the intermediate by democratic means; from Indian society, Mesopotamian, Phoenician, Ancient Rome, Europe and Americas. The Westphalia's treaty of 1684 brought about the formation of sizeable nation-states, particularly after the following congress of Vienna, the first part of the series of meetings held on the name of "concert of Europe" in 1815. Again, that created a new political boundaries for the numbers of cities and territories in Europe itself, *i.e.* Saxony city of Germany, France, some of the Italian cities, Netherlands, Duchy of Warsaw, etc. the congress was to identify the imbalance of power in Europe and to discuss the alternative solutions available. However, it is stood as a model of latterly international organizations, League of and United Nations. In a broader sense, more or less, the series of the held meetings served to democratize geopolitical demarcation in Europe.

The treaty has formed the normative structure or constitution of the modern world order. At the heart of the Westphalia's settlement, Europe's rulers agreed to recognize each other's right to rule their own territories free from outside interference. The codification in the doctrine of sovereign statehood has been there over a time. Meanwhile, it was only in the twentieth century, as global empires collapsed that sovereign statehood and with its national self-determination finally acquired the status of universal organizing principles of world order. The Westphalia Constitution by then had come to colonize the entire planet (Baylis *et al.*, 2008).

The process of democratization is rooted in the political struggle. Scholars like Dankwart Rustow believe that the process should contain well-entrenched forces of typical social classes. This struggle is likely to start because of the appearance of the new elite, which would unite diverse public groups into a combine battle. Each country has a different type of leadership, supporters as well as various peculiarities in the nature of this struggle. Therefore, the reasons and timeframes for this action are different, too (Rustow, 1973).

Samuel Huntington stated that, the increase of popular expectation of periodic and competitive elections, poor economic performances, which lead to legitimate loss of authoritarian regime, economic modernization through global economic output. This helped mostly less developed economies to address many changes in their structures, such as urbanization, education and rising of the middle class, is among the factor that expand breakthrough of democratization in many countries of undemocratic regimes (Huntington, 1991).

Parenthetically, the "third wave of democratization" synthesized by Huntington has gradually changed the map of the world since the late 1980s. The transitions in many Asian countries such as Philippines, Taiwan and South Korea preceded the dramatic collapse of communism in Eastern Europe and a new democratic system emerged in their places. These waves however, move to Africa and Middle East as well. Thus, this is strengthening democratic camp in international organizations and weakening the communistic block as alternative ruling ideology. Meanwhile, this evolution enables democracy and human rights to gain new status in the global level of reference for modern statehood and legitimate ruling. A number of democratic states rose after the collapse of Soviet Union and other communist regimes and end of Cold War respectively. Yet the current observation poses a question whether these states are truly democratic or the exercise of the real power still rests with autocrats.

Many studies on the process of democratization pay much attention on the concept of civil societies and their competencies to encourage the process of democratization and highlight its positive roles in transition from authoritarianism to sustainably democratic system of government. Hence, building an athletic civil society is perhaps precondition for democratization and consolidation of democracy especially in the third world nations. The suitable examples are recent democratic revolts in the Arab world, from Tunisia, Egypt, Libya, Syria, Yemen, to the state of Bahrain and so forth. According to Huntington, individual agents are very important in the transition to democracy, democracies created not by causes but by causers. To him, the transition was based on elite choice, participation, beliefs, and actions while subsequent consolidation was based on elite pacts and consensus.

Until recently, the roles that civil societies play in the Arab world are contrary to their counterparts in the other parts of the world where opposition political parties take clear position in attempting to extract democratic reforms from the authoritarian regime. In the Middle East and North African (MENA) region, both political parties and civil society organizations are relatively weak.

Despite being weak and passive, civil society organizations have become inevitable and primary instigators of change, besides; they also marginalize official political parties. In MENA region, the 2011 uprisings; Tunisia and Egypt were the recent paradigmatic instances. The rapid expansion of these demonstrations was of civil societies. Nevertheless, civil societies are estimated to have an impact on the political system setting in the whole region in the short period to come.

MONARCHISM AND DEMOCRATIZATION IN THE GLOBAL AND MOROCCAN PERSPECTIVES

Cardinally, the monarchy is no longer important after it has been considered a system that failed to sustain its prolonged existence for a longer period due to the autocratic type of its nature. But still the monarchy in many countries in Europe, Africa and Asia, led and becomes a doorway for democratization. In Western Europe, multiple monarchies do exist. Region-wide, these monarchies have very much contributed to democratization processes. That is what subsequently, known as 'Constitutional Monarchies'. In fact two of the founding-members of the European Coal and Steel Community, the body that would become EU later on, namely Belgium and Luxembourg are now among the constitutional monarchies. However, many of these monarchies are now enjoying full membership of the regional organization (European Union [EU]). Democracy champions one of the prime concerns of EU bidding countries are to be assessed. Nevertheless, throughout its enlargement process, from 1951 onward, the Union awarded full memberships to many European constitutional monarchies.

Those countries include Belgium, Denmark, Luxembourg, Netherlands, Spain, Sweden, and the United Kingdom (in pre-Brexit). Regardless of the types of these monarchies: constitutional, popular etc. but it's beyond doubt that somewhere between 16th and 19th centuries, if there was a system that seemed alternative to monarchy, it had been a system with no popularity compared to 20th and 21st centuries. Similarly, in Asia, countries like Bhutan from the south; Brunei, Cambodia and Malaysia from the southeast and Japan from the east, and of course, Morocco the only monarchy in North Africa, inject toward democratizing and act as catalysts for change in their countries' systems.

In Europe history shows that some conflicts of interests between church and state occurred. For instance in England, Henry VIII withdrawn from Catholic Church and established the Church of England after Catholic prohibited him to divorce his wife whose could not produce male heir for him. In Italy the new monarchy emerged after the incidence of 'Black Death'. Monarchy supports the middle class people and traders not only because of their needs to government intervention but also because they stand as strong and reliable source of taxes and revenues generation.

These heavy taxes, economic and political domination of the monarchs at that time coupled with awareness of the communities were among other reasons that alerted those monarchs and helped them to decentralize their powers to the elected body. That was long process carried out over the period of hundreds of years.

Categorically, in Bhutan for instance, in 1999 King Jigme Singye Wangchuck brought and pioneered wonderful reforms in the kingdom of Bhutan, the first of its kind in the entire history of the country. Through the new revised constitution presented publicly in 2005, King Wangchuck surrendered most of his powers to the cabinet ministers. Impeachment of the king by two-third of the majority in the national assembly was initiated; freedom of expression expanded, whereupon bans on televising and internet communications were lifted.

Tremendously, it was indeed successful contribution that left an utmost paradigm in the region. Importantly, some countries with mixture of monarchies as symbolic and parliamentarian democratic elected government *e.g.,* Japan, have more than one time responded positively in a situation where a democratic civil rule overthrown by military dictatorship or some other type of coup d'état. Despite being a country with monarchic regime (partially), Japan practically remains anathema to non-democratic system of government. For instance, in 1991 because of the coup in Haiti, Japan froze its Official Development Assistance (ODA) until 1994 when Jean-Bertrand Aristide was restored, whereupon ODA resumed in 1995 to the new democratic regime.

Foreign Aids of course motivate Moroccan consolidation, but the regime has already kicked off to move for more opening. Moroccan regime after many centuries has finally proved a litmus-test of its commitment to carry out transformation agenda in the country as early as the time between 1956 and 1960. The immediate first years of post-independent Morocco, though many experts observed what could be 'meretricious move' simply because what regime showed to outside world in documents was obviously different from reality. But it has also been learnt that, the Moroccan regime, regardless with many shortcomings that appear during this process, still some certain level of adaptabilities such as conscious will and readiness to process are seen through.

Until recently, Moroccan monarchy proves its seriousness on democratization through numbers of multiple activities such as inviting different political organizations to participate in political life of the country, freeing political prisoners, different constitutional reforms, changes in the *Makhzen i.e.* replacing the interior Minister, expanding the freedom of press and civil society organizations, and the biggest one is holding regular elections including the credible one of 2011, which allowed the Islamist party (PJD) to form a coalition government led first by Abdelilah Benkirane. Constitutional monarchy is also needs time to stabilize, but still some positive outcomes are witnessed, therefore, it is good beginning for Morocco.

Lise Storm stressed that in the last seven years, between 1990 and 1996, Moroccan regime managed to improve in human rights condition and revised two constitutions: 1992 and 1996 that has latterly come something of watershed in terms of political historical of the country (Storm, 2007: 54).

Moroccan monarchy seems to deliver this process through some three main areas namely political opening, constitutional modifications and human rights. There are also other forms in which monarchy tries to convey the same endeavouring message. Some of them of course, are successful and others encounter failure. Frankly speaking, each one of these categories is escorted by one or more reasons. Be it dual attempted coup d'état during the 1970s, widespread riots in the country or even international pressure groups.

ROLES OF THE MOROCCAN REGIME AND TRANSITION TO DEMOCRACY

In the last decade of his reign between 1990 and 1999, King Hassan II had tried to transform and simplify the living of ordinary

Moroccan persons. The King introduced political opening in Morocco after it has been stasis for many years. Apart from the tremendous efforts carried out by him as per 1999, still there were many initial programs unattended. The new international climate that came at the end of the Cold War strongly supported a wide range of democracy. That was considered as external pressure on Moroccan monarchy so that it can conform to the new trend mounted specifically in 1992 after European Parliament denied aid package because of poor performances in human right as mentioned above.

At domestic level, the drought factor instigated rural influx to the cities, which parenthetically, resulted to unprecedented levels of unemployment and discontent. Slow change increased support to the Islamist groups as the only alternative that the Moroccan peoples had, which also alerted the monarchy toward the danger of ignoring social disaffection.

As early as 1990s, the monarchy found itself in a very fragile position. Several different factors account for this phenomenon; probably the most important was the Gulf War, which considerably effect Moroccan politics. Three developments were of particular importance: first was the traditional opposition - dominated by the *Istiqlal* and the USFP - grew in strength as these parties came together in their shared opposition to the Gulf War, thereby also challenging the monarchy. Second was the Gulf War which resulted in political unrest, as the citizenry took to the streets of every major city on 14 December 1990 and demonstrated against the war as well as against the Moroccan authority for sending troops to the American basement in Saudi Arabia to pledge war against Saddam. It was driven by sole interest of the United States, which to them, was no less than dominating over Middle Eastern affairs. Third was partially a result of a general trend of Islamist resurgence in the Middle East, and partly as a result of dissatisfaction with the already existing channels of popular participations, an increasing number of Moroccans chose to join the Islamist movements, particularly Abd al-Salam Yasin's Al-Adl wal-Ihsan or Justice and Charity Society (Storm, 2007: 54).

In pre-Gulf War, Morocco has significantly achieved progressive changes in its democratization agenda including constitutional revisions. Thus, the monarchy however, had altered the title of the Kingdom regarding the type of its government from absolute to constitutional monarchy. Despite these popular improvements, the progress seems very much ephemeral as the permanent institutional pillars, which allow unrestricted power continues to rest with the King were missing. No doubt, the municipal as well as legislative polls were held on a regular basis, and with transparency.

Within the period of twenty years, 1990-2010, the Moroccan crowned heads have been at a crossroads in which importantly, very careful decisions were taken in sharing power in the country. In the constitutional reforms of 1992 and 1996; the power of the parliament was expanded only to be one of the most important parts and indicators toward the progress of Moroccan democratization. In due course, the parliament could vote on government and reviews its general policies, as it could also indirectly investigate the government's actions through commissions of inquiry, and dissolve a government through a motion of censure or vote of no confidence (Freedom House, 2006).

Peoples demonstrate their commitments towards democratization; but still the implication of the exercise has very less to do with their daily lives and day-to-day exercises. The monarch in the other side stands as generous for civil and political change (House, 2006).

During the 2003-04 King Muhammad VI has decisively actively moved to reform the family code. Notwithstanding the personal rights together with other major international conventions were substantially improved, the rate of human rights violations remained high since the Casablanca's catastrophic bombings in May 2003. Corruption is another chief issue that the grand process encounters. The Moroccan palace has been working for the priority of the rule of law immediately after the incumbency of Muhammad VI in 1999. The efforts are seemingly fruitless in yet another bombing in Marrakesh 28th April 2011, which left 17 foreign nationals dead whose were mostly Europeans.

IMPROVEMENT IN THE RIGHTS OF THE PEOPLE

Throughout many decades, human rights, violation and discrimination against minority were very much common in Morocco. These prejudicing activities were steadily slowing down by the efforts of the King Muhammad VI who launched Equity and Reconciliation Commission (IER) to deal with the previous grievances of tortured families who suffered in the 1980s. Addition to that, the King however, enacted official dialogue in 2001 on the issue of marginalized group, notably Berber culture. Since then, teaching of the Berber dialects and culture in the public schools has now become formal matter; to advance the status of the Berber in the country's spheres more than before, the dialect has been used in writing textbooks and television programs (Arieff, 2011: 14).

The IER was inaugurated in Morocco, and it was the first in its type in the entire Arab world. In August, 2007, more than 193 million dollars have been spent to compensate some 23, 676 victims including some individuals, who will be having special treatment, such as jobs and other chances that, they might have lost during their imprisonment time. The issue of human rights reforms has inextricable concern likewise the matter of disappeared people who have been vanished for their implication in military's attempts to the life of the monarch and in attempts to overthrow the government in 1971 and 1972. Large numbers of these peoples were either pro-Western Sahara or inhabitants of the Saharawi territory in the 1970s. The following appointment of Yousefi as Prime Minister in March 1998, has seriously promised to track over the previous cases, and tried to ensure such kind of disdain on the course of opposition never happen in future Morocco.

Interestingly, some tremendous attempts were taken by the Moroccan authorities to openly chance the political system within its spheres for greater participation in early 1990s, six years after

Morocco endorsed bicameral parliamentary system for the first time in its modern history. The previous unicameral parliament offered limited mechanisms for the representation of mass interests since those parliaments were dominated by indirectly elected political actors aligned with the monarchy (Ketterer, 2001: 7–8).

From 1998 till 2003, Yousufi's government has made remarkable gestures toward releasing thousand of political detainees; Michael M. Laskier (2003) showed that in the final two years of Hassan II's reign, and the Yousefi's government was already allowed to free many prisoners. Simultaneously leading exiled political opponents and/or their families were granted permission to come back to Morocco, and perhaps without changing their political sentiments as a prerequisite of their returning to their homeland. The guarantee includes Marxist activist such as Abraham Serfety and family of the late Mehdi *ben* Barka, who was killed in Paris during the 1960s over his political antagonism towards King Hassan II (Laskier, 2003).

CONSOLIDATION OF THE REFORMS

After returning back from exile, Muhammad V (born on 10th August 1909 in the city of Fez), was the Sultan of Morocco between 1927 and 1957, and ruled as King from 1957 to 1961. During his life, Muhammad V was one of the focal nationalists who have also fought and won Moroccan independence in 1956 from France. Muhammad V died on 26th February 1961 in Rabat. He was deported to Corsica and latterly Madagascar in 1951 over his rebellion against French occupation and returned in November 1955. The negotiation he made with French colonisers in March 1956 led to the full independence of Morocco. Muhammad V was deposed by encouraged and organized pro-French reactionary on allegedly account of supporting *Istiqlal* party, and for requesting to form self-government in Morocco during the 1950s. King Muhammad V was the first King dreamt about modern Morocco based on liberty and political participation.

Despite his commitments and struggles to achieve independence from France, which could equip Morocco to adopt parliamentary democracy, Muhammad V could not be able to provide constitutional institutions to ease parliamentary system in the country with regular elections. Though political parties were formed but their freedom was limited in which liberalization was seldom to identify their existence. Muhammad V managed to administer all of the governmental spheres. Above all, he dismissed the cabinet formed by *Union Nationale des Forces Populaires* (UNFP), the very party won the first post-independence elections in Morocco[1] and replaced it with a new enacted cabinet. Marina Ottaway and Meredith Riley (2006) argued that Muhammad V not only dismissed the cabinet, he consolidated power by rallying rural notables and security apparatus to himself.

KING HASSAN II: REFORMS CONTINUE

Hassan II's era started with the death of his father, Muhammad V in 1961. Hassan II was born on 9th July 1929, and was the first born-child to his father. Hassan II attended religious training centre in the palace itself, which longed for two years, and later on joined the imperial college in Rabat. King Hassan II graduated from the University of Bordeaux, France. Nevertheless, he also served as acting deputy prime minister during the reign of his father. While assuming the throne, throughout his reign, Hassan II has been introducing many positives and developmental achievements particularly in democratic reformation. A year after assuming throne, a royal charter was formed followed by a constitutional monarchy.

The new constitution provides that King should be central figure in the executive branch of the government. Albeit the parliament with bicameral legislation: Assembly of

[1] UNFP has separated from mainstream Istiqlal (Independence) party and formed a new title after Moroccan attainment of independence from France in 1956

Representatives and Assembly of Councillors; holds legislative power. Constitutional reforms were approved in 1970 after the 1963's legislative polls, in which royalists secured fewer seats. Over political dissent, Hassan II declared both executive and legislative branches of government under state of exception. The approved constitution of the 1970s cured up the frozen parliament, and held fresh elections, but still the government did not deal with the remaining adversarial contents, corruption and other malpractices.

Parenthetically, that was a hard circumstance for the then 32-year old monarch. After struggling to frame up the constitution followed by the elections won by opposition nationalists and leftist parties, the ideas which made them popular were derived from pan-Arab nationalism led by Jamal Abdel-Nasser of Egypt and socialism in Russia. Subsequently war broke between Morocco and neighbouring Algeria in 1963, many opposition leaders seemed to support Algeria over Moroccan monarch.

Soon after banning all political activities, the King ruled with backing of the security forces, tensions remained however. In 1995 riots rocked towns throughout the Kingdom, leaving many dead and many more missing (Amair, 2012).

According to Guilain Denoeux and Rhys Payne, King Hassan II showed a remarkable degree of adaptability over the course of his 38 years reign. He presided over a shift in the very relationship between state and society. The political opening began with a consultative phase characterized by the *Conseils Consultatifs*, in which broader elements of society were invited to participate in dialogue over public policy and reform movement. The king went on to oversee a release of political prisoners, constitutional reforms, and the inauguration of the principle of *alternance*, whereby the most popular opposition party was granted access to the post of prime minister in 1998 (Denoeux and Payne, 2003: 17).

During the 1970s, King Hassan II was confronted by different issues, which traditionally might thwart the success of the already-started process of reformation. Those issues include expanding of Islamism that was among the top agendas to be dealing with; legalizing opposition parties to participate in the elections, though their political freedom and power were limited simply because of the created division, which undermine any possible threats. Meanwhile, these groups lacked enough political power to confront the interests of the palace.

Above all, the most significant reform that Hassan II tried to achieve during his life was the "Family Code" (the *Mudawwana*) *Mudawwana* is an Arabic word literally means "written documents", and is the title of Imam Malik's first jurisprudent Book. In Morocco, the term used as set of law under the Islamic *Shari'a* that contains rights and responsibilities of Muslim individuals pertaining to the interaction between among themselves at family level, such as marriages, divorces, kinship, inheritance and so forth).

Mudawwana reformation soon becomes controversial task. It influenced many *Ulama'* (the highly intellectual class of Muslim scholars) and chanced them to discuss such reformation keeping in mind political will. This improvement seemed very much difficult in previous time. King Hassan II has addressed the issue of reforming the *Mudawwana* several times during the early years of his rule, but his attempts lacked substance and real intention until the colossal changes in the world, such as the disintegration of the Cold War divide and calls for political liberalization and democratization at the end of the 1980s and beginning of the 1990s. It has become clear that the autocratic regime of Hassan II would not survive without addressing and changing its quasi-democratic and quasi-pluralistic political system allowing the political arena to be more inclusive, rather than exclusive. All of these developments concomitantly led to a revived interest in the reform of the sacredly ossified *Mudawwana*.

Consequently, in 2004, after a long historic struggle of more than one decade *Mudawwanat al Usra* emerged in a modern and revolutionary form (Zvan, 2007: 5). Politically, somewhere in 1998, King Hassan II has openly invited the opposition groups to work shoulder-to-shoulder in forming historical transition to democracy for the first time in the past 38 years. Hassan granted the post of Prime Minister to Abdur-Rahman Yousefi, who was opposition leader. Many experts believe that this opening was of great value not only on political sphere but also on economy too.

In the early 1980s, Moroccan economy was sick and thus needed lot of systematic reformations. The first attempt was said to be Structural Adjustment Program (SAP) which has been launched in 1983. The state sought to redress its slide toward bankruptcy by working out an agreement with the International Monetary Fund (IMF) that further constrained spending on debt-ridden public sector. The austerity programs however, watered down and postponed as hope for private investment failed to materialize to the degree needed to jumpstart rapid economic growth. Underemployment continued to soar, reaching an estimated 22 percent of the work force in 1999. The growing pockets of the poor in the bidonvilles that sprouted up around the large cities; were cause for concern as the state was increasingly unable to provide for their welfare (2003:4).

DEMOCRATIZATION PROCESS IN THE POST-HASSAN II'S ERA

The 1999 marked the year when the throne of a Moroccan palace passed to Muhammad VI through the means of inheritance after his 70-year old father passed away. During his administration, King Hassan II played a key role in the Middle East peace process, and become a staunch ally of the United States. He had also become a very important figure in the Gulf War, by mobilizing troops as part of Morocco's coalition against Saddam Hussein's invasion of Kuwait (Campbell, 2008). Whereupon succeeding his father, King Muhammad VI continued to give a certain degree of consideration to the process of democratization in Morocco with attentive consideration. Just like Hashemite in Jordan and al-Sabah in Kuwait, those recognized such movements and translated them into action through the modernizing monarchical power, rather than transferring ultimate political authority into the hands of elected representatives.

King Muhammad VI from the very beginning introduced his 'action station' to the wave of reformation. Under his stewardship, Morocco has taken a number of steps to expand political pluralism, liberalize public life, and improve its human rights record. This process watched and supported by Morocco's allies in Europe and the United States, who are eager to see Morocco become a model of a democratic and moderate Muslim state, in sharp contrast to the failures of American-endorsed Middle Eastern democracy projects in Iraq and the Palestinian Authority. Apart from political liberalization and trying to include many significant changes in modern Morocco, the positive indications in the new king, Muhammad VI's reign include linkage between the Democratic Association of the Women of Morocco (ADF) and government (Campbell, 2008).

Practically, in September 2002 elections, thirty seats reserved for women in the parliament. Regarding to the less qualitative education coupled with unemployment, many believe to be a challengeable factor to the young Muhammad VI. The new King according to Patricia, education and unemployment are key to his long term strategy for Morocco, although he was a bit bewildered about how, and where to start, while urging tax payers to pay their dues in order to fund the treasury. He has also set up a special fund to which affordable citizens can donate money that used for poverty programs. However, much of the Moroccan middle class struggles to get out of economic difficulties (Patricia, 2008).

Two decades passed over the leadership of King Muhammad VI, as entering to the third one, the king together with other Arab leaders witness political uprisings, demonstrations and upheavals, which shook down some of their beefy regimes. To escape the possibility of masses movements as such on 9th of March 2011, Moroccan monarchy, according to Alexis Arieff, gave nationally televised speech in which he promised a range of reforms to the political system of the country. The King has effectively appointed ad hoc commission to draft proposals for constitutional reforms. These proposals concerned much about what previous regime notably ignored like political freedom, job opportunities to the young graduates, etc. In early June 2011, the commission has submitted the proposed reforms in which it consulted with political parties, labour unions, business associations, human rights groups, and others.

The King moreover, expressed his certainty that the constitutional proposals include the resolution of the Western Sahara dispute (Arieff, 2011: 01). Arieff added that the major political parties have spelled out their support for the draft; they also urged their supporters to vote for such proposals. The parties who announced their satisfaction with the current action taken from the palace includes the Moderates Islamist opposition Justice and Development Party (PJD). The party nevertheless, acclaimed the process as "important advance," albeit, Justice and Charity Organization (JCO) since from the grass-root of its foundation refuses to recognize King as the Commander of the faithful, (*i.e. Amirul Mu'umineen*).

The new strategies followed by the Moroccan palace in translating the ambitious dream of unity, equality and justice in the country were provincial visits to mostly non-Arabs tribes *i.e.* Berber. Lise Storm quoted Cembrero justifying that during his first year on the throne, Muhammad VI had spent a large amount of time travelling around the country in an effort to win the approval of the population by showing his commitment to Moroccans at all levels of the society and in all the country's regions.

Eventually, that earned him the nickname al-*Jawal*-the mobile, a word commonly used for pre-paid mobile phone cards. By early 2001, however, it had become evident that the King's strategy for winning popular support, which had worked so well during the first year of his reign, had begun to backfire as his promises of reforms failed to materialize (Storm, 2007).

KING MUHAMMAD VI, MORE DEMOCRATIC MOROCCO?

During his first days on the throne, King Muhammad VI was known as 'King of Poor'. Though some of the tactics used by him to attract common Moroccans were not direct to the point, but the young Muhammad reaffirmed his zeal to win popularity throughout Morocco. Thus, this is seen as another step to realize utmost process of liberalization. Kingdom of Morocco developed a kind of expanding chances for Moroccan society to participate and take part in the reforming behaviour of the state in various sectors.

King Hassan II was the one who for the first time, developed the idea of bicameral legislature in Moroccan parliament. This action continues to maximize massive political participation from different political orientations: secularists, Islamists and nationalists. Similarly, King Muhammad VI's ascending to the power seems 'grist to the mill'. The King launched several techniques of engaging Moroccan society for the formation of new democratic Morocco that could aptly go hand-to-hand with the modern day without exaggeration or lagging Islamic norms, which stands as total way of life for Muslims behind.

Marina Ottaway and Meredith Riley, make it clear that during the King Hassan II, dialogue and improvement in the administration of elections led to better relationships between the palace and most political parties. That is because political groups are closer to society through politicians who, during campaign normally promise to take responsibilities of satisfying basic and necessary needs of the people if elected. Accordingly, Hassan II would have been able to bring about the most visible political accomplishment of this reformist period in which '*alternance*' successfully seen through. Instead of installing palace's parties to form the government as usual, King Hassan II neutralized the palace's parties and allowed USFP leader to form the then government (Ottaway and Riley, 2006: 6). Contemporarily, the relationship between the palace and society is increasingly becoming positive and systematic. Again, Moroccan authorities seem to be all-aware of the bulky responsibilities that they have to fulfil for betterment of the people and for better Morocco. King Muhammad VI announced and celebrated his own royal wedding in public. This happened for the first time in the history of modern Morocco. This development served a clear message that from now onward, the renewal process of social justice and equality started replacing the old restricted attitude of the palace toward its subjects.

It was very damnedest behaviour to televise Muhammad VI's marriage to then 24-year old Salma Bennani, a computer engineer graduate from Fez. This is tremendous development for Moroccans because in the past, issuing any notice regarding family or any other related matter in traditional Morocco was considered a crime against the honour of the King and Royal family. Afrol-News, the online News cable, reported that, it's highly risky to make any statements on a matter related to the members of Sharifians royal family. But during the king Muhammad VI things unusually started taking different direction. Muhammad VI broke with the Royal traditions by announcing his marriage event, while his father, the King Hassan II's marriage was announced instead of keeping it secret after Latifa (*i.e.* second wife), conceived.

Furthermore, the freshly unexpected move was seen through the royal family, sent a signal, not only to Moroccan people, but also to the world, that the Moroccan monarch is moving forward and becoming more responsible with moderately standard behaviours than remaining as angle sent from the heaven (Afrol-News, 2002). Fitness of the King Muhammad VI shines the palace by attracting realization of the society that the king is a ruler and protector, who comes down closer to us, listens to grievances we have, seeks our opinions in matters concerning our beloved country regardless of being the chief of all Moroccans.

The New York Times remarked on him as popular, a king who looks more like a movie star than monarch does. On a recent tour to some parts of the country, countless numbers of the peoples on streets showed their jubilant mode and welcomed him. Schools were closed, ancient markets shut down and entire families trooped to the roadside to see the young king, who arrived in their locality (The New York Times, 1999). While in office, King Muhammad VI keeps focusing on new concepts of authority. He made popular calls to improve the condition of the majority Moroccans who live in poverty and other social malaises. However, the king conciliated Moroccans *via* several factors including taking another direction for wider political participation (Whitney, 1999).

Seemingly, Morocco's aware that the social and economic condition are in devaluation; the King has understood that he can no longer continue to tackle these issues effectively, and retain legitimacy in the eyes of the public by turning a blind eye to the political domain (Colombo, 2011: 8). However, the February 2011 demonstrations were the key points that perhaps compelled the regime to convince the people that it will engage the direct participation of the citizens in decision making, security and other domestic issues. The king however, portrayed his desire to reformation through a massive referendum that has brought about the new package of revised constitution in order to placate down potential anxiety from the people during the Arab Spring, which dominated and emerged as the main event in the entire Arab world throughout 2011. This has very much helped in paving the way for long live monarchy.

The Arab spring has resulted in some significant improvements in human rights in Morocco (Pollack *et al.,* 2011: 200). In the first weeks of the spring, the King freed close to one hundred political prisoners and invested more power in the National Council for Human Rights. He nevertheless appointed the founder of the Moroccan branch of Transparency International, Abdesselam Aboudrar, president of the national anti-corruption agency. Secondly, the level of public participation in the reform process has been positively increased compared to the previous time. Thirdly, the new constitution takes major steps forward to providing a balance of powers in which the Moroccan parliament has real authority. The prime minister has expanded powers, but the parliament will also find the threshold much lower for forming an inquiry commission and presenting a motion to censure or remove the government, compared to the absolute majority required before.

During the crises (in North Africa), although Moroccans somehow, demanded greater reform, but never called for removal of the King Muhammad VI neither they required toppling down the regime, which indicates that the relations between the state of Morocco and its subjects, especially in the reign of King Muhammad VI was smooth (Zisenwine, 2011: 104). The country had previously experienced political reform and as a result had a general trust in the monarchy as an agent of change rather than one of repression. The relationship between society and monarchy is more or less something depending on how and where the regime places itself in the society. Many observers praised King Hassan II for his several attempts to liberalize Morocco, and put more emphasis on Middle East and North African issues particularly with relation to democratization of the Arab world in general.

Regarding to the issue of decentralizing power, King Hassan II, as the top spiritual leader of the country and commander of the faithful, not allowed surrendering all the powers that normally hold by the commander of the faithful and reign without governing (Campbell, 2003: 41).

In shaping political development alongside connections between the monarch and Moroccan elites, Saloua Zerhouni (2004) explained that the monarchy is the main component of the political system and the centre around which all political actors revolve. During King Hassan II for instance, power manipulated to safeguard the king from an oppositional threat, as so as much King Hassan managed to keep changing situation and political challenges using repression, and consensus. While King Muhammad VI on the other hand, has applied the so called "reinforcement of the centrality of the monarchy," through a more liberal style, guaranteeing his predominance in politics. The act of institutionalization of the royal powers has a dual function. On one side, it is an important tool for controlling the elite by seeming to give them a voice in decision-making as well as regulating their integration into the political system, while on the other side, it is a way of affirming the pre-eminence and the efficiency of the monarchical institution (Zerhouni, 2004: 62).

CONCLUSION

Despite number of challenges and shortcomings encountering by Moroccan authorities, yet the democratization agenda of the country is considered a point of reference in the entire region. Morocco is the only country with monarchic (constitutional) system of government in the entire North Africa, and less affected by the recent Arab springs. Although the authoritarian type of leadership it has, supposed to attract more tension even if the uprisings are not given any consideration, but due to the regime's commitments, the country was survived with small injuries. The potential matching/mismatching attitudes of democracy and Islam however, attract attention of many scholars in the Arab and Western world. Morocco of course, becomes one of the targets point. Some scholars like Lise Storm, see Morocco as non-qualified to be considered democratic one.

REFERENCES

Afrol News (2002). "The Morocco's Royal Wedding, Breaks without Traditions". [Online: web] Accessed 28 December 2011 URL: http://www.afrol.com/News2002/mor005_royal_wedding.htm

Arieff, A. (2011). "Morocco: Current Issue". [Online: web] Accessed URL: http://www.fas.org/sgp/crs/row/RS21579.pdf

Baylis, John *et al.* (2008). The Globalization of World Politics, New York: Oxford University Press.

Campbell, Patricia J. (2003). "Morocco in Transition: Overcoming the Democratic and Human Rights Legacy of King Hassan II". *African Studies Quarterly*, 7(1): 41.

Colombo, S. (2011). "Morocco at the crossroads: Seizing the Window of Opportunity for Sustainable Development". [Online: web] Accessed URL: www.ceps.be/ceps/download/5490

Dworkin, R.M. (1999). Freedom's law: The Moral Reading of the American Constitution, London: Oxford University Press

Freedom House (2006). Country at the Crossroads, Country Report-Morocco: Washington DC.

Guilain, Denoeux and Rhys, P. (2003). "Democracy and Governance Assessment of Morocco". [Online: web] Accessed 20 May 2011 URL:http://pdf.usaid.gov/pdf_docs/PNACX727.pdf

Held, David (2006). Models of Democracy, Chicago: Stanford University Press.

Huntington, S.P. (1991). The Third Wave: Democratization in the Late Twentieth Century. Oklahoma: University of Oklahoma Press.

Ketterer, James P. (2001). "From one chamber to two: The case of Morocco". *Journal of Legislative Studies*, 7(1): 3–19.

Laskier, Machael M. (2003). "A difficult inheritance: Moroccan society under King Muhammad VI". *Middle East Review of International Affairs*, 7(03): 15–16.

Ottaway, M. and Riley, M. (2006). Morocco: From Top-Down Reform to Democratic Transition, Carnegie Paper No. 71, Carnegie Endowment for International Peace, Washington, D.C.

Rustow, Dankwart A. (1973). "Transition to democracy toward a dynamic model". *Journal of Comparative Politics,* 2(3): 337–363.

Storm, L. (2007). Democratization in Morocco: The Political Elite and Struggles for Power in the Post-independence State, New York: Rutledge.

Whitney, Craig R. (1999). "Popular New King Has a Goal: A Modern Morocco", The New York Times, New York.

Zerhouni, S. (2004). "Morocco: Reconciling Continuity and Change". *In*: Volker, Perthes (*ed.,*) Arab Elites: Negotiating the Politics of Change, Colorado: Lynne Rienner Publishers, Inc.

Zisenwine, D. (2011). "The Emergence of Nationalist Politics in Morocco: The Rise of the Independence Party and the Struggle against Colonialism after World War II". *African Studies Quarterly*, 12(4): 104.

Žvan, K. (2007). The Politics of the Reform of the New Family Law (The Moudawana), Ph.D. Thesis, London: University of Oxford.

9

The Debate Around Freedom of Expression: Need for Deliberative Democracy in India[1]

Tamanna Khosla[1]*

ABSTRACT

The right to freedom of speech as one of the basic human rights is enshrined in the main international human rights documents. Freedom of speech (synonym of freedom of expression) is an inseparable element of a democratic society. Whether the society is democratic or not can be defined by the factor of independent press and mass media. The Constitution of India provides the right to freedom given in Articles 19, 20, 21 and 22, with the view to guaranteeing individual rights that were considered vital by the framers of the Constitution.

Key words: Deliberative democracy, Freedom of expression, Collective decision making.

[1] Department of Political Science, Delhi College of Arts and Commerce, Delhi University

**Corresponding E-mail*: tamannakhosla@gmail.com

[1]Republished from intellectual resonance.

INTRODUCTION

The right to freedom of speech as one of the basic human rights is enshrined in the main international human rights documents. Freedom of speech (synonym of freedom of expression) is an inseparable element of a democratic society.

Article 19 of the Universal Declaration of Human Rights (UDHR) lays down: "Everyone has the right to freedom of opinion and expression; this right includes freedom to hold opinions without interference and to seek, receive and impart information and ideas through any media and regardless of frontiers".

Article 10 of the European Convention on Human Rights (ECHR) maintains: "Everyone has the right to freedom of expression. This right shall include freedom to hold opinions and to receive and impart information and ideas without interference by public authority and regardless of frontiers. This Article shall not prevent States from requiring the licensing of broadcasting, television or cinema enterprises".

IS RIGHT TO PRIVACY ABSOLUTE

However, certain areas need to be discussed here. The first issue which must be looked into is whether this right is absolute. There is a difference of opinion amongst public intellectuals. Certain scholars like Pratap Bhanu Mehta believe that the right is not absolute. For example, according to him, some version of hate speech will need to be prohibited in any democracy. Certain kinds of violent pornography could also be regulated. Of course, at one level, this will have to be determined on a case–by-case basis. But writers like Salman Rushdie believe it is absolute in nature. According to him, countries like the US would emphasize on the need for absolute freedom of expression. This is the great strength of the First Amendment, that is, allowing even hateful things to be said, it helps you to see where the enemy is, it assists you to demolish arguments. There is also the powerful argument which is that you do not remove from society terrible ideas by banning them. You in fact increase their power by giving them the power of taboo.

Thus while Mehta believes in case-to-case analysis, Rushdie believes in absoluteness of the freedom. Lately in India democracy is under stress.

LIBERAL GROUPS *VS* FRINGE GROUPS

Be it certain political groups against Valentine's Day celebration, Taslima Nasreen's visa issue, Rushdie's attending the Jaipur literary fest, M.F. Hussain's paintings, the Bajrang Dal being against nude painting in Delhi, ban on women's rock band in Kashmir or ban of *Vishwaroopam* in certain States. All of them hit out at the democracy's basic sensibilities. There is a sense of anarchy prevailing in Indian democracy. Secularism, it can be easily said, has been understood the other way round. While it is fine to consider respect for all communities, one of the ways we understand secularism is also as the state being neutral in religious matters, the Church and state being separate. This, however, is not true of secularism's definition in India. But surely the state in India can make positive interventions. The state needs to reconcile the right of expression with the right of communities to get hurt. One must debate, for example, whether an individual writer's right to be victimised by fringe groups needs to be protected or the right of communities to get hurt on issues such as a cartoon of the Prophet or a movie like *Innocent Muslim* needs to be defended.

RIGHT TO ABSOLUTE *VS* LIMITED PRIVACY: THE CASE OF US AND INDIA

Here one must understand the base of one's democracy. In the US the right to expression is defended in an absolutist sense; this is because individual rights are the basic feature of the US Constitution. But in India despite the defence of individual rights, it also gives the right to culture to its religious communities. Thus when there is a contradiction between the individual right to freedom and right to culture, the political climate in the country has defended the right to culture. Multiculturalism as against liberalism is being defended in our country. While India is moving towards economic liberalism the contradictory issue is that it is scared to liberalise its public space. Countries like China have gagged the voice of democracy and also the right of minorities like Tibet's residents. India too is blamed for muzzling the voice of the people of Kashmir, or trampling the rights of people in the North-East. It has been blamed for inadequate understanding of the Maoist uprising and using violence against them. A democracy cannot function if the voice of any individual or group is suppressed.

What one needs to understand is that India must cultivate an environment of deliberation amongst its different religious communities. When some members of the AIMPLB called Rushdie for debate that could be seen as the sign of a growing democracy. Any issue can be tackled when mistrust is removed from the mindset of the conservative sections as well as writers and artists who ask for free speech. We need to distinguish ourselves from the religious forces which terrorise the masses to behave in certain ways, be they Muslim, Hindu, Christian or any other force. Otherwise, it will be a very sad state for democracy in India.

NEED FOR DELIBERATIVE DEMOCRACY

In a deliberative democracy people need to reason out to each other for the respective positions they take and an understanding needs to be evolved amongst them[2]. For example, if it is the issue of a painting or a novel, then the state could accommodate deliberations between the painter or the writer and the groups claiming to be hurt by the content of the piece of work. Thus both could be made to understand their specific viewpoints. For instance, Rushdie

[2] Gutmann Amy and Thompson Dennis (2004). Why Deliberative Democracy? Princeton, Princeton University Press.

pointed out several times that people who criticised him had themselves never read his novel! Hence the conflict is largely because of misunderstanding between groups or individuals. This can be deflated by the development of trust and mutual understanding between them[3].

Democracy thus is quintessentially a manner of collective decision-making in which everyone participates on an equal footing and no one's interest or feeling gets hurt. Deliberation thus believes that conflicts are best addressed and provisionally resolved by actual deliberation, the give and take of argument that is respectful of reasonable differences. The deliberation recommended here is not speculative but oriented towards decision-making. Deliberation calls upon people to acknowledge the moral status of their own positions and also to acknowledge the moral status of those reasonable positions with which they disagree. When there is as yet no universally justified resolution, the people who fundamentally disagree may insist as a matter of social justice that conflicting perspectives be fully considered by a deliberative process of decision-making. Democracies like India can aid deliberation between diverging groups. Our moral understanding of many side-issues like articles, movies, legalising abortion is furthered by discussion with people whom we respectfully disagree, especially when these people have cultural identities different from our own[4].

But India is not a deliberative democracy[5] right now because of the sheer size of our democracy. Thus the democracies in India and the US are at different levels. While the US can defend even the Ku Klux Clan's right to hate speech, the same might be difficult in a culturally plural country like India, which has seen animosities between majorities and minorities. India still has to wait for a level of democracy where free speech won't hurt sentiments on

[3]Ibid

[4]Levy Ron and Graeme Orr (2016). The Law of Deliberative Democracy, Routledge

[5]ibid

religious issues and where religious groups are suspicious of each other's concern. The recent case of Togadia and Owaisi's hate speeches reflect that the state needed to enter the arena to reduce further aggravation of the situation. However, saying this does not mean that the individual rights of citizens need not be protected. While cultural rights are important, these rights should not be allowed to relegate individual rights to the periphery. For example, any kind of violent pornography needs to be regulated. Some kinds of art must be regulated. But that doesn't mean that these should be banned. Individuals have the right to be offended and criticise an article, a novel, movie or any work of art but banning them in a democracy is no solution. It would make India no different from China or any of those Islamic countries which have strict regulation of the internet, novels or the kind of art being produced.

CONCLUSION

Reconciliation between Right to Individual and Right to Culture

Thus if India needs to progress as a democracy, we have to see how the right to expression of the individual and the right of the cultures can be reconciled. And that would surely require dialogue in society on how far the freedom of expression should go. Artists, writers, creative experts on the one hand and the orthodox sections of different communities on the other have to seriously deliberate on this issue for the future of democracy in this country[6].

SUGGESTED READINGS

Gutmann Amy and Thompson Dennis (2004). Why Deliberative Democracy? Princeton, Princeton University Press.

Levy Ron and Graeme Orr (2016). *The Law of Deliberative Democracy*, Routledge.

Chappell Zsuzsanna (2012). *Deliberative Democracy, A Critical Introduction*, Palgrave Macmillan.

[6] Ibid

10

Factor Analytic Study of Political Violent Behaviour (Thuggery) Scale (Povibes): Development and Evaluation

MFON E. INEME[1], ABAYOMI A. OKEDIJI[1], HELEN O. OSINOWO[2] AND CHINWEIKE F. UDEAGHA[3]

ABSTRACT

Thuggery is a contemporary social problem. It affects the social, political, and economic life of any society. Nigeria's experience has been worrisome, long-lasting, and tends to persists despite attempts to curb it. Thuggery, an antisocial behaviour because of its notoriety and resilience has, assumed new dimensions on daily basis which has made it difficult to stem its occurrence in the Nigerian political scene. Since all human behaviours have psychological dimensions, this study made use primarily of a psychological approach by developing and validating a scale which measures the tendency of Nigerians to be involved in or sponsor thuggery. The study was conducted in three sequential phases – IDI and FGD were used in phase one to develop the items guided by the DSM-IV criteria for conduct and antisocial disorders, experts' judgment constituted the

[1]Department of Psychology, University of Uyo, Nigeria.

[2]Department of Psychology, University of Ibadan, Nigeria.

[3]Department of Psychology, Imo State University, Owerri, Nigeria.

**Corresponding E-mail*: mfonineme@yahoo.com

second phase, and administration of the raw items and statistical analysis using SPSS form the third phase. The study therefore aimed at developing an instrument that is culture-sensitive to measure the proneness to political thuggery among Nigerians with the intention of forestalling the crime by offering psychological intervention to those detected to be prone to this form of antisocial behaviour. It was basically a survey and samples were drawn from Uyo metropolis.

Key words: Factor analytic study, Violent behaviour, Politics, thuggery, Scale development, Scale evaluation, IDI, FGD, Breaking of law, Hostage taking, Intimidation, Theft, Vandalism, Nigeria

---

INTRODUCTION

Globally, political leaders are often accused of thuggery, *i.e.* making use of thugs to achieve their political ambitions. Thuggery involves the use of people, especially supporters, who, in turn, make use of violent measures to assist their "masters" to achieve their ambitions or vengeance. At its best, thuggery is a criminal behaviour (Hornby, 2001); this implies that it is punishable by law. A thug has been described as someone, especially, a criminal who is brutal and violent (Encarta, 2009). Oxford Dictionary of Current English (1998) defines it simply as a violent act or behaviour by ruffians. It is simply the criminalization of politics. When politics is criminalized, it is left in the hands of ruffians, thugs and hooligans, because the good people are scared away (Lawal, 2011). Howell (2004) defined thug politics the tireless repetition of misleading facts designed to depict an opponent as personally despicable and in regard to governance as dangerous to physical and spiritual life of a nation. From the foregoing, it is observed that thuggery is synonymous with violence and hostility. Violent or aggressive behaviour have been known to have not only cultural roots but also genetic explanations (Coccaro, Bergeman, Kavoussi and Seroczvnski, 1997); thuggery may not be left out of this.

In Nigeria, the term has become very popular in the diction of the citizens and other inhabitants especially during the few years of civil rule. Expectedly, thuggery in Nigeria has its own peculiarities in terms of its cause, practice, and effect. Commenting on thuggery in Nigeria, Obasanjo (2002) asserted that we fight, and sometimes shed blood to achieve and retain political power because for us in Nigeria, the political kingdom has, for too long, been the gateway to the economic kingdom. This statement, in the words of Lawal (2011), captures the content and context of political thuggery and violence in Nigeria. The statement demonstrates how blood is being exchanged for political power in Nigeria. Slightly on the contrast, the American thuggery tends to be characterized by threat letters, passage of bills to weaken unionism, etc (Cline, 2011), though, it cannot be said to be totally void of physical violence.

Worthy of note also is the fact that thuggery is not strange to the Nigerian polity. According to Lawal (2011), the annals of the Nigerian politics reveals that "Nigerian politics have since independence, been characterized by thuggery and violence. This trend is not a phenomenon of recency; thuggery, brutality and violent political behaviour have been with us for the past four decades. This makes politics to be viewed as a dirty game, favourable only to thugs and hooligans in Nigeria. Consequently, Nigeria's politics manifest in acrimony, assault, assassination, intimidation, harassment, maiming, kidnapping, and killing. Immediately after independence the politicians, in an attempt to capture, exercise, and retain power within their regional settings involved themselves in various acts that were politically immature, unwise, and disastrous. They adopted a style that was antithetical to democratic tenet and good governance. They recruited, trained and empowered thugs to harass, intimidate and victimize perceived political opponents and opposing views against their political ambition. This culture of thuggery has been imbibed and sustained as part of the country's political behaviour since independence to the present moment.

Seeing the activities involved, it could be readily concluded that a certain segment of the society-the youths-would constitute better recruit for thuggery. Youths here refer to males and females between the ages of 15 and 25 years. Globally, people within this age range are known to be prone to violence and crimes. But it is obvious that behaviour exhibited at the age of 18 years and above does not just start at that age. It certainly could have started earlier in life though, may be, not pronounced and so not noticed. Put differently, the potentials and tendencies for such behaviors could be accounted for by earlier, childhood experiences. This, therefore, makes it necessary to study, in younger people the tendency or predisposition to becoming a thug; with the intention of curbing the thuggery tendency and preventing its full fledge manifestation. One of such ways is to develop an instrument that could possibly measure or detect thuggery tendency among Nigerian youths which could predispose them to thuggery by making them ready recruits for such criminal behaviour.

Activities of Political Thugs

In actual political scenes, thuggery involves verbal abuses, intimidation, physical fight or fist, snatching of election materials, kidnapping/hostage-taking, arson, and killing. To carry out their activities, thugs often make use of bats, whips, broken bottles, knives/machetes, guns, and other harmful weapons. They are known to illegally possess legally restricted weapons – an act which further incriminates the behaviour. Thuggery is an act characterized by rudeness, hooliganism, touting, intimidation and harassment. It is a behaviour that contradicts peace, harmony and co-existence among groups (Lawal, 2011). To enhance their activities, thugs often engage in the use and abuse of psychoactive substances.

Purpose of Political Thuggery

Political thuggery is an illegitimate and violent means of seeking political power with a view to subverting national opinion for parochial ends through self imposition (Lawal, 2011). Resorting to thuggery could be explained as an indication of frustration by a politician who has a false belief that he/she should win in an election, even against the will of the people. This is in line with the Frustration-Aggression Theory which holds that hostile (emotional) aggression becomes eminent and rises when there is some interference with an expected attainment of a desired goal (Dollard, Doob, Miller, Mowrer and Sears, 1939; Berkowitz, 1989). Nigerian politicians appear to be easily frustrated by real or perceived interference to their achieving their political ambitions; correspondingly, they quickly resort to aggression and violence against the real or suspected source of interference. It is also resorted to when politicians perceived that what they consider their rights would be denied them. Political thuggery may also become a culture, used and justified by many politicians – in this case, it is used even when it is not necessary; all these appear to be Nigeria's experiences and realities.

Effect of Thuggery

As is characteristic of every criminal behaviour the world over, many human lives and property have been lost to thuggery. People have been humiliated, maimed, or deformed. For instance, it was reported that deadly election-related violence in northern Nigeria following the April 2011 presidential voting left more than 800 people dead. The victims were killed in three days of rioting in 12 northern states (Human Rights Watch, May 16, 2011). It was also reported that roughly 17,000 people fled their homes in eight northern Nigerian states and Red Cross treated 360 people who suffered injuries – all following election violence (CNN, April 19, 2011). The citizenry has lost confidence in the electoral processes for this one reason. It has been used to perpetuate discrimination against certain groups. Thuggery has made criminals (thugs, hooligans and the incompetent) to become leaders while the good, competent people are scared.

And it has been said to be the bane of women's participation in politics (Lawal, 2011). With this, politics appear to be exclusively men's affairs.

PURPOSE OF THE STUDY

The purpose of the study is to develop a valid, reliable, and sensitive psychological instrument (scale) for measuring the tendency or proneness of Nigerians to be involved in, or sponsor political thuggery.

Need for the Scale

From independence in 1960, the Nigerian political system has suffered a lot of setbacks attributable to the activities of political thugs. Lives and property have lost, people have been maimed, others have been kidnapped, elections have been postponed or cancelled, wrong and incompetent people have made to emerge as leaders, and Nigeria has lost her place of pride and dignity among community of nations, all due to activities of these hoodlums (thugs). Law enforcement agents have made a number of arrests and detentions, the criminal justice system through the courts has punished with different penalties. Yet thuggery activities before, during, and after elections have persisted. There is therefore a need for psychological intervention since thuggery, like other criminal behaviours, has psychological undertone. Procedurally, the first thing to do is to measure the tendency of such behaviour among Nigerians youth (who are often used as thugs) and the politicians themselves. To achieve this feat (of objective measurement of the thuggery tendency among Nigerians), there is need for an instrument which is culture-sensitive and population-specific, hence the need to develop and validate an instrument within the Nigerian culture. So far, there appears to no indigenous psychological instrument that directly measures thuggery tendency among Nigerians; a few however measure hostility generally and majority are foreign (*e.g.*, Buss. and Perry,

1992; Buss and Durkee, 1957). The scale will also serve as a sensitive therapeutic and research instrument for psychologists and other behaviour scientists, and a screening instrument for policy-makers and law enforcement agents. Generally, the scale shall provide a valid and reliable tool for assessment of thuggery tendency, prevention of thuggery and intervention planning.

LANGUAGE

The scale is designed in English language, the Nigerian lingua franca. The items are constructed using daily used English words common in the Nigerian society for easy understanding among target population – Nigerians.

USAGE

To measure the tendency or likelihood to be involved in or sponsor political thuggery.

METHOD

This study was conducted in three consecutive phases as follows:

Phase One (Development of Items)

Design

This phase of the study was cross-sectional survey utilizing ex-post facto design.

Setting

The setting for this phase of the study was Uyo metropolis. Uyo is the Capital of Akwa Ibom State; Uyo is situated at 5.03° North latitude, 7.93° East longitude and 196 metres elevation above the sea level. The population of Uyo is 309,573 (National Population Commission, 2006).

Sampling method

Purposive sampling method was used in this phase of the study; only partisan politicians, active card-holding members of political parties, political scientists, and active unionists were sampled for this phase of the study. Uyo was purposively selected because of the high rate of political activities characterized by thuggery, kidnapping, and other violent behaviour as at the time of this study.

Participants

A total of 15 residents of Uyo, Akwa Ibom State Capital participated in this phase of the study. They were 13 males and 2 females; their ages ranged from 21 to 48 years, with a mean age of 32.4years. They were all Nigerians.

Instruments

In-depth interview (IDI) guide and focus group discussions (FGD) guide were used to guide the interviews and discussions with participants, a tape recorder, pen, and paper were used to record the conversations. Copies of the IDI and FGD Guides were presented to the experts – 1 clinical psychologist and 1 political scientist for validity. Each ended up with 7 items.

Procedure

In-depth interview (IDI) sessions were held with 2 politicians who had contested elections, 3 active card-holding members of 3 political parties, 2 political scientists, 2 street boys, popularly known as "area boys", and a focus group discussion (FGD) with 4 male and 2 female undergraduates of the University of Uyo who were actively involved in student unionism. Each IDI lasted an average of 45 minutes while the FGD lasted about 55 minutes. The purpose of the study was explained to each participant and the intention to use tape recorder was disclosed at the beginning of each session; their consents were sort and only volunteers participated. At the end of the IDI and the FGD, regular themes emerged. Those themes, together with the DSM-IV criteria for conduct and anti-social disorders (American Psychiatric Association, 2000), and the relevant personality traits that described the behaviours relating to thuggery, motivation for thuggery and violent behaviour as discovered from scientific literatures (Barlow and Durand, 2002), aided the development of the initial items for the scale.

Result

At the end of the phase, 53 initial items were developed for the scale.

Phase Two (Experts' Judgment)

Design

This phase of the study was cross-sectional survey utilizing ex-post facto design.

Setting

The setting for this phase of the study was Uyo metropolis. Uyo is the Capital of Akwa Ibom State; Uyo is situated at 5.03° North latitude, 7.93° East longitude and 196 metres elevation above the sea level. The population of Uyo is 309,573 (National Population Commission, 2006).

Sampling method

Purposive sampling method was used in this phase of the study; only experts in human behaviour (clinical psychologists, social psychologists, organizational psychologists and political scientists) were sampled for this phase of the study. Uyo was purposively selected because of the high rate of political activities characterized by thuggery, kidnapping, and other violent behaviour as at the time of this study.

Participants

A total of 6 human behaviour experts resident in Uyo metropolis in Akwa Ibom State Capital participated in this phase of the study. They were 4 males and 2 females; their ages ranged from 39 to 51 years, with a mean age of 43.3 years. They were all Nigerians.

Instrument

The instrument for this phase of the study was the initial version of the intending scale consisting of the 53 raw items developed at the end of the first phase.

Procedure

The initial 53 items were presented to the 6 experts – 2 clinical psychologists, 1 social psychologist, 1 industrial/organizational psychologist, and 2 political scientists) for face and content validity. With their independent contributions, judging the suitability and wording of the items, the initial scale ended up with 42 items which were used in the third phase of the study.

Result

At the end of the second phase, 42 initially valid items were obtained for the scale.

Phase Three (Administration of Raw Items)

Design

This phase of the study was cross-sectional survey utilizing ex-post facto design.

Setting

The setting for this phase of the study was Uyo metropolis. Uyo is the Capital of Akwa Ibom State; Uyo is situated at 5.03° North latitude, 7.93° East longitude and 196 metres elevation above the sea level. The population of Uyo is 309,573 (National Population Commission, 2006).

Sampling method

Purposive sampling method was used in this phase of the study; only partisan politicians, active card-holding members of political parties, political scientists, and active unionists were sampled for this phase of the study. Uyo was purposively selected because of the high rate of political activities characterized by thuggery, kidnapping, and other violent behaviour as at the time of this study.

Participants

Four hundred and twenty-eight (428) residents of Uyo, the Akwa Ibom State Capital participated in the study. They were 321 were males while 107 were females; their ages ranged from 19 to 52 years with a mean age of 33.48 years. They were drawn from the Uyo metropolis. Of the total population, 308 (72%) were from the South-South, 92 (21.50%) from the South-East, and 28 (6.54%) from other parts of the country; 296(69.16%) were students of tertiary institutions, 41 (9.57%) were self-employed, 46(10.74%) were civil servant, and 45 (10.51%) served private firms/individuals. They were all Nigerians.

Instrument

The instrument used in this phase of the study was a structured questionnaire with three sections. Section A contained the demographic variables/ bio-data of the participants, section B contained the initial 42-item scale validated by experts, and Section C contained Buss-Durkee Hostility Inventory (Buss and Durkee, 1957) which was used to ensure convergent validity with the new scale.

Procedure

The instruments were administered to the participants in their classrooms, offices, sit-outs, and halls of residence. Necessary and required explanations were given to the participants and all their questions were attended to. Each participant was allowed an average of 72 hours to complete the scale. A total of 450 copies of the instrument (initial 43-item scale) were administered to participants but 19 could not be retrieved while 3 were discarded due to improper completion. With this, 428 copies were used for the analysis.

Statistical analysis

The responses of the participants were subjected to reliability and factor analyses using SPSS Version 15.0.

Results

At the end of the analyses, 39 items were found reliable (each having at least 0.3 Cronbach's coefficient) with general Cronbach's Alpha co-efficient of 0.91. The factor loading (analysis) revealed 6 sub-scales finally arranged as follows: Sub-scale 1 (items 1-6), measuring tendency for breaking of rules with Cronbach's coefficient of 0.51, Sub-scale 2 (items 7-13), measuring tendency for hostage taking with Cronbach's coefficient of 0.72, Sub-scale 3 (items 14-19), measuring tendency for intimidation with Cronbach's coefficient of 0.68, Sub-scale 4 (items 20-30), measuring tendency for physical violence with Cronbach's coefficient of 0.77, Sub-scale 5 (items 31-36) measuring tendency for theft with Cronbach's coefficient of 0.51, and Sub-scale 6 (items 37-39), measuring tendency for vandalism with Cronbach's coefficient of 0.60. The final version of the scale also has a convergent validity of 0.32 with Buss-Durkee Hostility Inventory. With these, the final outcome was a 39-item valid and reliable scale with the name: Political Violent Behaviour (Thuggery) Scale (POVIBES). These imply means that the final version of the scale contains 39 items: 6 items measuring the proneness to breaking of rules, 7 items measuring proneness to hostage taking, 6 items measuring proneness to intimidation, 11 items measuring proneness to physical violence, 6 items measuring proneness to theft, and 3 items measuring proneness to vandalism (**Appendix A**).

Examples of items

Breaking of rules

1. I do not like any body controlling me.
2. I do not like where there are many rules or laws.

Hostage taking

1. A wicked politician can be arrested and detained any where for peace to reign.
2. I believe that arresting and keeping a rich man is better than armed robbery.

Intimidation

1. A political opponent can be threatened with any weapon but not killed.
2. Any body that goes into politics must get ready to be insulted

Physical violence

1. I can use any weapon to defend my political office.
2. No political campaign era can start and finish without bloodshed.

Theft

1. Government property does not belong to any body; taking it is not crime.
2. I sometimes tell lies to get what I want.

Vandalism

1. I notice that when I am deprived of my right, my regards for human lives and property is reduced.
2. To me, setting fire to a house is a way of showing aggression.

PSYCHOMETRIC PROPERTIES

Scoring

The Political Violent Behaviour (Thuggery) Scale (POVIBES) is prepared in a Likert-type format, scaling 1-3, and showing the varying degrees of a respondent's proneness to being involved in or sponsoring thuggery. All items are directly scored. The minimum score is 39 and the maximum score is 117.

Norm

The norm of the Scale is 63.4, established at 2 standard deviations above the mean. Scores below the norm show low tendency to becoming a thug or sponsoring thuggery while scores from the norm and above show high tendency to becoming a thug or sponsoring thuggery, and call for psychological intervention.

DISCUSSION / CONCLUSION

A 39-item psychological instrument for measuring the tendency to involving in or sponsoring thuggery among Nigerian has been developed following a scientific procedure. With the development and validation of this Scale, there now exists an objective means to measure the extent to which Nigerians are prone or favourably disposed to political thuggery. The Sub-scales also revealed the different components of the Nigerian political thuggery *i.e.* the possible activities involved in by political thugs in Nigeria. These have implications for forensic psychology; intervention packages for Nigerian political thugs should take into cognizance the different possible behaviour of these members of the society. Other crime experts, legal practitioners, other members of the criminal justice system, and law enforcement agents may now have to watch for any these components while dealing with political thugs and political thuggery situations. The emergence of the different sub-scales indicating a variety of activities that political thugs may possibly engage in, is confirmation of the fact that criminal do not specialize; given the chance, one who commits one crime would commit another. However, there is need to interpret the scale into Nigerians some languages since the illiterates are often quick recruits for political thuggery. It could also be re-validated for use in other parts of the country and other African countries.

Appendix A

Copy of Political Violent Behaviour (Thuggery) Scale (POVIBES)

Items	*Bking Rules*[1]	*Hos Tak*[2]	*In-tim*[3]	*Phy Vio*[4]	*Thf*[5]	*Van*[6]	*Cron. Coef*[7]
1. I believe that politics and violence must always go together.							
2. I do not like any body controlling me.	.457						
3. I do not like where there are many rules or laws.	.447						
4. I do not see anything wrong helping a leader to succeed provided I get some reward.	.501						
5. In this life, deceit is often necessary.	477						
6. There are days I miss appointments just to stay friends.	.499						α=0.51
7. A wicked politician can be arrested and detained any where for peace to reign.		.677					
8. Arresting and keeping an opponent for a ransom is better than killing him/her.		.703					
9. I feel that political ambitions should be upheld above anything else.		.710					
10. I feel that the unemployed youths can make some money from the arrest and money detention of the rich but selfish men in the society.		.689					
11. I believe that arresting and keeping a rich man is better than armed robbery. (Host. Tak)		.510					

Table: (*Contd...*)

Table: (*Contd...*)

Items	*Bking Rules[1]*	*Hos Tak[2]*	*In-tim[3]*	*Phy Vio[4]*	*Thf[5]*	*Van[6]*	*Cron. Coef[7]*
12. If I have my way, any opponent picked up for political reason should not be let go without a fee.		.609					
13. It is pardonable if a politician dies in the custody of opponents; after all they are all the same.		.578					α=0.72
14. A political opponent can be threatened with any weapon but not killed.			.677				
15. Any body that goes into politics must get ready to be insulted.			.647				
16. I can frighten any body to get what I want even though I may not inflict any physical injury.			.545				
17. I can shout at any body who tries to disturb my political leader.			.634				
18. I often use threat or intimidation to get my way when people try to hinder me.			.632				
19. No one can shout at me and get away with it; I must shout back.			.588				α=0.68
20. I can have sexual affairs with someone I love whether the person likes it or not.				.677			
21. I can initiate or start a fight to save myself or get what I want.				.767			
22. I can use any weapon to defend my political office.				.701			
23. I do not really feel guilty fighting especially if that will help me to get some benefits.				.699			
24. I feel political party supporters should defend their parties at all costs.				.545			

Table: (*Contd...*)

Table: (*Contd...*)

Items	*Bking Rules*[1]	*Hos Tak*[2]	*In-tim*[3]	*Phy Vio*[4]	*Thf*[5]	*Van*[6]	*Cron. Coef*[7]
25. I sometimes go to train on how to fight.				708			
26. If a dog or cat makes my surrounding dirty, I feel like hitting hard.				.589			
27. If a stronger person wants to suppress me, I can use any weapon to save myself.				.754			
28. No political campaign era can start and finish without bloodshed.				.767			
29. The death of a political opponent can be facilitated where necessary.				.520			
30. To my mind, bullying other people is not a big crime.				.776			α=0.77
31. Government property does not belong to any body; taking it is not a crime.					.600		
32. I sometimes tell lies to get what I want.					.578		
33. To my mind, snatching of election materials is normal in my country.					.577		
34. When I have the opportunity, I take things that do not belong to me if I find them useful.					.609		
35. While fighting with someone, I can snatch his/her property or money to make him/her feel he/she does to me.					.599		
36. Money meant for political purposes can be used for something else.					.601		α=0.61
37. I notice that when I am deprived of my right, my regards for human lives and property is reduced.						.588	

Table: (*Contd...*)

Table: (*Contd...*)

Items	*Bking Rules*[1]	*Hos Tak*[2]	*In-tim*[3]	*Phy Vio*[4]	*Thf*[5]	*Van*[6]	*Cron. Coef*[7]
38. If seriously provoked by an opponent, I can destroy any nearby person or thing in reaction.						.509	
39. To me, setting fire to a house is a way of showing aggression.						.599	α=0.60

[1]Breaking of rules [2]Hostage taking [3]Intimidation [4]Physical violence [5]Theft [6]Vandalism [7]Cronbach's coefficient.

REFERENCES

American Psychiatric Association (2000). Diagnostic and Statistical Manual of Mental Disorders Fourth Edition Text Revision (DSM-IV-TR), pp. 645–650. Available at http://www.dsm.psychiatryonline.org/doi/book/10. Retrieved on 06/06/2013

Barlow, D.H. and Durand, V.M. (2002). *Abnormal Psychology: An Integrative Approach (3rd ed.).* Australia: Wadsworth.

Berkowitz, L. (1989). Frustration-aggression hypothesis: Examination and reformulation. *Psychological Bulletin,* 106(1): 59–73.

Buss, A.H. and Durkee, A. (1957). An inventory for assessing different kinds of hostility. *Journal of Consulting Psychology,* 21: 343–349.

Buss, A.H. and Perry, M. (1992). The aggression questionnaire. *Journal of Personality and Social Psychology,* 63: 452–459.

Cline, A. (2011). *Democrat Thuggery in its Worst Form.* Available at http://www.spectator.org/achieves. Retrieved on 11/03/2011.

CNN Wire Staff (2011). *Widespread Election Violence Erupts in Nigeria.* CNN News. Available at http://www.cnn.com/2011/04/19. Retrieved on 06/06/13.

Coccaro, E.F., Bergeman, C.S., Kavoussi, R.J. and Seroczvnski, A.D. (1997). Heritability of aggression and irritability: A twin study of the Buss-Durkee aggression scale in adult male subjects. *Biological Psychiatry: An Official Journal of the Society of Biological Psychiatry,* 41(3): 273–284.

Dollard, J., Docb, L., Miller, N.E., Mowrer, O. and Sears, R. (1939). Frustration and aggression. New Haven CT: Yale University Press.

Howell, R. (2004). *Political Thuggery in Vogue.* Chicago: L and T Press Ltd.

Human Rights Watch (2011). Nigeria: Post-Election Violence Killed 800. Available at http://www.hrw.org/news/2011/05/16. Retrieved on 12/06/2013

Microsoft Encarta (2009). 1993-2008 Microsoft Corporation.

National Population Commission (2006). National Census Report. Available at http://www.population.org.ng. Retrieved on 12/06/2014.

Lawal, T. (2011). *Political Thugsgery and Violence in Nigeria: The Bane of Women Participation in Politics*. Available at http/www.2ez2find.com.

Obasanjo, O. (2002). 42nd Nigeria Independence Anniversary National Broadcast. *Tell Magazine,* 41.

11

Future Establishment of Competition Among Political Parties in Uzbekistan

SANJAR SH. SAIDOV[1]*

ABSTRACT

This scientific analyzes article the place and role of political parties in a society. Multi-party system and political competitive factors among political parties are set forth. The participation of political parties is analyzed as an essential institution of civil society as well as national and international experience. Moreover, the author shows scientific outlook about political parties' start on competition, struggle of political ideas and ideology during pre-election campaign and electoral activity.

Key words: Political party, Civil society, Electoral campaign, Political competition, Electorate, Political discourse, Ideology, Parliament.

[1] Senior Scientific Research-Worker of Uzbekistan State University of World Languages, Chilanzar-18, House 10a, Apt. # 5, Tashkent, 100153, Uzbekistan.

**Corresponding E-mail*: s.saidov.uz@gmail.com

As it is known, one of the main principles of establishment of democratic republic and civil society is formation of state government bodies through public election and citizen participation in state and society issues directly or through representatives, whom they elected. In this matter, political parties, which is one of the indispensable institutions of civil society play important role, as they function as a "bridge" between state and society.

Political party is civil voluntary union participating in governing of public issues, and also which is established based on unanimity of interests and aims, striving for realization of political will of a particular sphere of society in establishing of state government bodies[1]. Political parties represent political will of different layers and groups and take part in forming state government through their representatives, who are elected in a democratic way[2].

Political parties, initially, effect on decision making process according to their electoral interests, political ideology and position and through their representatives engage in setting public controlling over central and local executive branches of state.

Thus democratization of state control, law priority accomplishment in society and formation of own view point of political parties in effective provision of human rights and freedom in state, having capacity of moving forward programs aiming at development of state and society, ability of conducting meaningful discussions with its political opponents (other political parties), in a word, establishment of inter-party competition and developing multi-party system in state political system is plays an important role.

Only multi-party based social-political relations create favorable conditions in order to build civil society. The factors such as the position of political parties in the society in establishment of state representative and executive bodies, its participation in these processes, peoples attitude towards elections based on the multi-party system, "ideas struggle" among political parties are becoming essential indicators marking today's democracy.

As world experience show, political parties' role and importance increase in country's "transition period". Their competition in social-political life is also going on increasing through essential tendency. In this process transformations also occur in the place of political parties in society, *i.e.* party changes from ordinary supporter union to representative democratic institution. Multi-party system also serves as debate area in solving problems and issues in social-political lives of a state and to come to a reasonable compromise[3].

If considering world experience in this matter dispute and mutual struggle among parties escalate especially on the eve of elections. Political parties try to achieve leadership in upcoming election processes and aim at promotion their ideas widely among electorate.

Comparative analysis of pre-election propaganda in Western and Eastern countries

Western countries	Eastern countries
Political system of Western countries	Political system of Eastern countries
Political ideology	Personality/ Individual
Political party	Political party
Personality/ Individual	Political ideology

Fig. 1: Arranged on the basis of comparative analysis pre-election campaign in Western and Eastern countries

As it is shown from the table, political ideology dominates in the political system and pre-election campaigns of developed

Western countries. That is to say, it is paid great attention to the ideology, unique state and society improving program of the political party. Electorate also votes for the alternative programs. Therefore proportional election system is applied in most European countries. In the next positions political parties and personal qualities of a candidate are taken into consideration.

Whereas in Eastern countries' election process status of the individual stands as a main point. Identity of the candidate, his place in social life, his position, even charisma of his are considered as main factors, which are interesting to electors. In this process political ideology takes the last place.

This comparative table is arranged on the basis of analysis of election processes, scientific analyses of activity of political parties and multi-party system. It reflects only scientific outlook of the author.

Pre-election processes, political parties' participation in parliament and their competition in regular activity are also based on such indicators. Electorate (voters), who is the main the subject of political processes, political parties, state and civil society institutions are established and conduct their activity according to this system.

As it can be shown from the comparative analysis, there are a lot of discrepancies in political thought, social-political systems of Western and Eastern societies. It can be considered as one of the main duties standing in front of society to study them scientifically and to maintain analyzing.

The political discourses conducted regularly among parties, which are discussed in solving actual contemporary social-political and social-economic issues, is of great importance.

Political discourse is political process establishing communicative relation among political parties (as well as among other civil society institutions)[4]. Discourses in their turn are political means, which are controlled by political leaders, conducted to special audience and having its special language. Political discourse serves as a main factor in discussing internal and external policy of a state by political parties in election campaign, in debate processes related to state and society along with analyzing social-political processes.

Mass media plays an important role in processes of political parties' debating. As it is seen from the developed countries' experience, TV debates, briefings and press conferences are held not only during pre-election campaigns, but also regularly about actual social-political and economic issues.

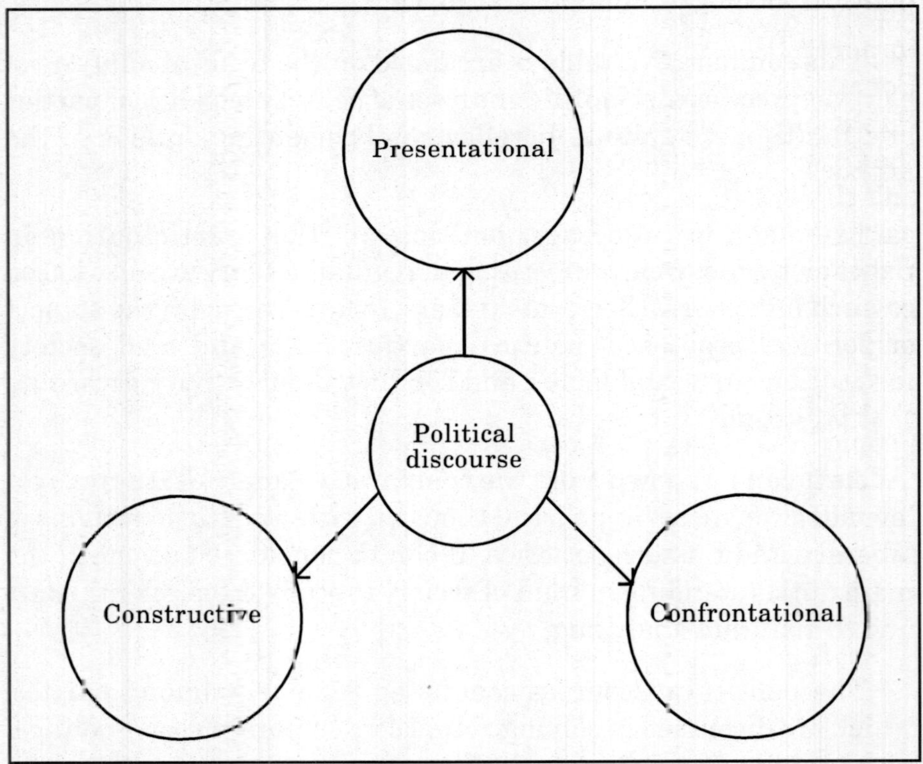

Fig. 2: Forms of "Political discourse": Arranged by comparative analyzing of political processes.

The vital aim of political discourse is not only to classify of current condition in a simple manner, but also to convince the electorate of own ideas and thoughts, to create positive image and to arise motivation in audience. As of these, political discourses are met in the forms of presentational: presenting their ideas and programs, constructive: showing their position towards current authority (or political party), *i.e.* putting forward of their position, *confrontational*: functioning as an opponent to current authority (or political party).

During the independence years there have been set up organizational, legal and institutional bases on establishing multi-party system and improving efficiency of its activity. In this regard, the system of legal arrangement of political parties' activity is important to emphasize in our country. For instance, the Constitution of the Republic of Uzbekistan, the laws such as "On Public Organizations", "On Political parties", "On the elections of the Oliy Majlis of Uzbekistan", "On the elections of region, district and city Councils of People's deputies", "On financing of political parties' activity", and the Constitutional Law of the Republic of Uzbekistan "On Renovation and further democratization of state governing, and increasing the role of political parties on state modernization" should be distinctly emphasized.

In the political arena of Uzbekistan has four political parties - People's democratic party of Uzbekistan, Social democratic party "Adolat" ("Justice"), Democratic party "Milly Tiklanish" ("National revival") and the Movement of entrepreneurs and businessmen - Liberal democratic party of Uzbekistan.

- The People's Democratic Party of Uzbekistan (NDPU) is the first political party formed after independence in 1991. It can be called the legal successor of the former Communist Party of the Republic of Uzbekistan. The party was established on November 1, 1991. According to the official data, the total number of members is about 360,000 people, and 11,162 primary organizations of the party which are functioning all over our Republic. The head of the central council is Khatamjon Ketmanov. The main goal of the party, described in the NDPU regulations, is the material and spiritual well-being of the person, family, and the reliable provision of equal opportunities, constitutional rights and civil liberties, the protection of honor and dignity, the peaceful life of people regardless of their nationality, social status, political convictions and religion. The Party's publication media is the newspapers "Uzbekiston Ovozi" and "The Voice of Uzbekistan";

- The Social Democratic Party of Uzbekistan "Adolat" - was founded on February 18, 1995 at the founding congress. The highest organs of the party: the Congress, the Political Council, the Presidium of the Political Council. Chairman of the Political Council - Narimon Umarov. The current Action Program of the Adolat SDP was adopted on December 17, 2005. The total number of members is over 75,000. There are 2.536 primary party organizations. The party's publication media is the social and political newspaper "Adolat". The main goal of the party is to build a legal democratic state that meets the interests of all nations and nationalities living on the territory of Uzbekistan, including establishing social justice in the society, ensuring the rights and freedom of the individual, creating a moral and enlightened civil society;
- The Democratic Party of Uzbekistan "Milliy Tiklanish" was formed on June 20, 2008 by the decision of the united congress on the basis of the merger of the Democratic Party of Uzbekistan Milliy Tiklanish and the Fidokorlar Party. Chairman of the party Sarvar Atamuratov. The main goals of the party are: to create favorable conditions for the growth of national self-consciousness, to form and strengthen a sense of national pride of citizens of the Republic of Uzbekistan, devotion and love for the Motherland, uniting the patriots of their country, mobilizing intellectual and creative potential for serving for Uzbekistan and raising its international authority, making an effective contribution to the cause of patriotic education of youth in the spirit of respect, love and pride for their Motherland. The total

number of party members is more than 108,000 people. The party's publication media is the political newspaper "Milliy Tiklanish";

- The movement of entrepreneurs and businessmen - the Liberal Democratic Party of Uzbekistan (UzLiDeP) - was established on November 15, 2003 by the initiation of the country's President I. Karimov. The main goal of the Party is - consolidation, unification and coordination of owners in their activities. The leader of the party is Sodikzhon Turdiyev. The members of the party are more than 160,000 people. The party's publication media is the socio-political newspaper "XXI asr", (the 21st century - from the Uzbek one) established on November 18, 2003.

Necessity of establishing healthy and constructive competence is increasing among parties on step-by-step development of parliamentarism and development of election system and further democratization of state governing in Uzbekistan. The factor of competence among parties should be paid highly attention to parties' rotation in government for effective performance as of being inseparable part of it.

If we analyze it as an example of Uzbekistan, the formation of political competence among the parties in the country is advancing gradually. The participation and particular experience gained during election processes of political parties in elections for the Oliy Majlis and local Councils of people's deputies in 1994, 1999, 2004, 2009 and 2014 years serve to enhance their activity.

Moreover, interventions referred to the participation of political parties in elections, to show its power, to strengthen the role of political parties in modernizations of Uzbekistan is being established and come into realization[5;72]. The issue of improving efficiency of political parties is regarded as actual matter in the activities of representative bodies of the authority. We can say that the activity of fractions in the parliament, their position from processes of making law projects to control-analysis assignments are the hallmark of political competence.

As the first President of the Republic of Uzbekistan Islom Karimov claimed: "Figuratively speaking, especially in parliament activity, it should make a regular appearance of competence of ideas and programs, each party should achieve their aims and targets through such a competence... The more intense and the stronger the competence among different political fractions in Legislative Chamber, the firmer and the more stable will be the guarantee of the realization of each parties' ideas and duties, which reflects interests of society's particular sphere"[5;81].

In broad sense, establishment of multi-party system provides pluralism of thoughts, serves as a main factor in democratization of the society. As the President of the Republic of Uzbekistan Sh. M. Mirziyoev emphasized: "Strengthening of multi-party system, increasing the effect of political parties in the lives of state and society, the duty of forming healthy competence environment among them is today's crucial task"[6].

Furthermore, there are several other issues in social-political modernization of the society and further democratization of state governing system, as well as intensification of the role and the position of political parties. They include:

- There is a necessity of refining effectiveness of political parties, using of new and innovative methods in working with electorate and converting parties into literary representative democratic institution.
- It should be effectually used methods and methodologies experience formed in world's developed countries during the pre-election propaganda processes. On this matter it is better to use various briefings, debates, public relations campaigns and etc.
- Time itself requires reformation of "analytic centres" (Think tanks), which regularly carries out research about issues of political parties in actual social-political and social-economic issues on forming state and society, makes proper and constructive programs on solutions of the problems and participates in realization of them in our life.

REFERENCES

[1] The Law of the Republic of Uzbekistan (1996). "*On Political Parties*", 337-I – edition.

[2] The Constitution of the Republic of Uzbekistan (2011). T., Uzbekistan. Article 60.

[3] Политическая стратегия европейской буржуазии в XX веке. Ч. 1.—М., 1990 С. 97–112. (Political Strategy of the European Bourgeoisie in the Twentieth Century (1990). P.1 - M., P. 97-112).

[4] Язык и наука конца XX века. Сб. статей. М.: РГГУ, 1995. С. 35-73. (Language and Science of the Late XX Century (1995). Complex of articles. M.: RSUH, pp. 35–73.

[5] Каримов И.А. Жа?он ин?ирозининг о?ибатларини енгиш, мамлакатимизни Б:72 модернизация ?илиш ва тара??ий топган давлатлар даражасига кўтарилиш сари. T 18., (Karimov I.A. To deal with the consequences of the global crisis, the country towards modernization and rise to the level of developed countries. T 18., p. 72).

[6] Ўзбекистон Республикаси Президентлигига номзод Шавкат Миромонович : (The Program of the Candidate to the President of the Republic of Uzbekistan Shavkat Miromonovich Mirziyoev) http://www.uzlidep.uz/uzc/content/uzbekiston-respublikasi-prezidentligiga-nomzod-shavkat-miromonovich-mirziyoevning-tarzhimai.

12

Children and Adolescents' Digital/Social Media Usage

UMANA ANJALIN[1,2]*

ABSTRACT

Adolescents and children of today spend most of their time online. Using their favorite gadgets like the smartphones, tablets, or laptops they indulge in social networking while remaining online. These millennias, or in other words, popularly known as the Generation Y, are known to communicate online most of their times they remain awake. They even sleep with their phones next to their beds. Many of these expressive individuals, however, are not fully aware of digital literacy and the etiquette of digital citizenship. As a result, many of them fall into the traps of negative impacts caused by the social media such as online harassment, cyberbullying, sexting, identity theft, depression, internet addiction, sleep deprivation, etc. The growing concern with children and adolescents' safety issues give rise to the question of parental monitoring. The monitoring of children's online activities has some positive as well as negative

[1] Doctoral Candidate, College of Communication and Information, School of Advertising and Public Relations, University of Tennessee, Knoxville, USA

[2] Assistant Professor, Department of Business Administration, University of Asia Pacific, Dhaka, Bangladesh

**Corresponding E-mail*: anjalin.umana@gmail.com; uanjalin@vols.utk.edu

sides. This chapter introduces the millennial generation's online behavior with social media, the concerns associated with that, and the issue of parental monitoring.

Keywords: Children and adolescents, Social networking, Social media, Online harassment, Cyber bullying, Digital footprint.

INTRODUCTION

This Information Age has exposed today's younger generation to the state-of-the-art computers, smart gadgets, high-speed internet, and other technologies and these children and adolescents have integrated all these expertise in their everyday lives. Even the task of submitting assignments in handwriting is so very old school for many of the digital generation (Millennials) now as they type up book reports and present their findings using software packages like the PowerPoint[1]. Not only the computers, smart gizmos and the internet, today's digital generation's favorite pastimes now also are the use of the new media, popularly known as the social media. Using the social networking sites is one of the most common activities of today's adolescents and children[2].

HOW THE SM SITES ARE USED BY THE SOCIAL MEDIA SAVVIES

The *millennials* are the digital citizens. Tablets and *smartphones* are their favorite gadgets to keep them entertained while on the go. Nowadays 81% of teens, while being online use the social media (SM). This generation also reveals a lot more about themselves *via* this new media than ever before[3]. The benefits of children's, preadolescents', and adolescents' usage of social media include enhancing communication, maintaining social connections (with friends/classmates/peoples of shared interests), and even honing technical skills[4][5][6]. However, concerns remain how this generation could become digital literates and good digital citizens as there is much more to digital citizenship and social media usage than getting a good score in a game involving angry fowls! This chapter will present a discourse on the children and adolescents' contemporary usage of social media and will discuss some of the issues that could be crucial matters of concern regarding the young generation's usage of the new media. Some discussions regarding a number of guidelines that could be followed to keep the children and adolescents' safe online will be suggested.

SM plays an important part in friendship *via* social media in the lives and emotional well being of the youth, preadolescents (especially in the developmental periods), adolescents[6]. The children, preadolescents, and adolescents mostly use SM for entertainment and communication[2]. It presents them myriad opportunities for connecting with friends, classmates, and people with shared interests[2]. Other benefits of SM include: having a sense of emotional association[7], remaining in touch with the existing peers[8], fostering new ones[4], maintaining relationships as a antidote for loneliness[9], having emotional support while transitioning to college[10], gaining educational benefits[6]. However, many parents' concerns regarding the usage of the social media hover around the unhealthy use of this media and the other potential problems[2]. Before delving deeper into the concerns regarding the younger generation's contemporary practice and possible harm from careless of using the social media, looking into the social media usage statistics will be giving a better understanding and a background about the concerning issues involved.

Social Media Usage Statistics

This might sound cliché, but social media is here to stay! Here are some of the recent statistics. On an average, children are getting access to smartphones by the age of 10[11]. 75% of teenagers own a cell phone, and 25% use them for social media, 54% use for texting, 24% use them for instant messaging[12]. Children studying in grades 4 through 6, are below Facebook's required age of 13, are the users of the Facebook platform[13]. According to a result published from a poll in 2009, 22% of teenagers logged on to their favorite social media site more than 10 times/day, and more than half of adolescents logged on to a social media site more than once/day[14]. Therefore, a substantial part of this generation's socialization and emotional development is happening while being on the Net and cell phones.

The Infant Media Exposure and Some Related Risks

The internet indispensably has now become a part of a child's life. More than half use social media by the age of 10[14]. Infant media exposure and use mostly plays a detrimental role in early child development beginning at infancy which has been linked to symptoms of lower levels of in attention of reading, and lower levels cognitive, language development, and educational achievement[15][16][17][18]. The majority of parents of young infants today expose their infants to television and videos. Research shows that in the low-SES families, most infants were exposed to television and videos. Median overall exposure while awake was 120 minutes, with approximately half of the exposures to programs not intended for young children among which, very little exposure to programs specifically directed toward infants[18].

Parents usually try to ingrain the behavior in children at a very young age never to talk to strangers. However, with social media in a tablet, smartphone, or a PC, children suddenly find themselves reading or hearing words from millions of strangers across the world! Parents usually try to ingrain the behavior in children at a very young age never to talk to strangers. However, with social media in a tablet, smartphone, or a PC, children suddenly find themselves reading or hearing words from millions of strangers across the world!

SOME CONCERNS REGARDING THE YOUNG GENERATION'S USAGE OF SOCIAL MEDIA

In addition to the pros of using social media, there is also a crucial issue of keeping children safe online. The prime concern of children and adolescents' social media use is their vulnerability. Other concerns regarding the possible risks include: child cyber bullying, negative online comments, harassment, kids giving into peer pressure, internet addiction and sleep deprivation, privacy issues like children's sharing unnecessary information *via* the Internet, the prevalence of pedophiles who trap children *via* the social media, postings of inappropriate photos, sexual experimentation, and "sexting," etc. There is a burning issue of monitoring children's social media activities and limiting their screen time. Should the parents be paying more attention than what they are doing right now regarding their children's social media activities? What may be the effects of monitoring children's internet activities? What may be the after effects concerning adopting a passive state (*i.e.* the parents' not monitoring /not paying attention regarding the children's Internet activities)? The pros and cons concerning all these will be discussed with evidence from scholarly articles, internet sites, and video footages, and then a stance will be adopted at the end of the discussion.

The Possible Risks from Negative Impacts of Social Media

The stories of negative impacts of social media on children are not at all hard to find. There have been plenty instances of:

- Verbal abuse of child cyberbullying[19][20]
- Children's sharing unnecessary or too much information *via* the Internet[21][22]
- Unintentional disclosure[23]
- Posting inappropriate photos, sexual experimentation[20]
- Privacy issues and "sexting"[24]
- Prevalence of the network of pedophiles that trap children *via* the social media[21]
- Negative online comments, harassment, and kids giving into peer pressure[2]

- Negative relational experiences[6]
- Facebook depression[2]
- Jealousy[25]
- Internet addiction and sleep deprivation[26][27], etc.

Below is the discussion of some of the risks emanating from the negative impacts of social media:

Cyberbullying

Cyberbullying could be characterized as a forceful, deliberate act or conducts by an individual or a group of individuals, utilizing electronic media, continuously and over a period, against a recipient who is not able to safeguard him/herself[28]. It has been argued that the adolescents' level of social and emotional maturity, and their limited capacity to self- regulate make them especially vulnerable to peer pressure[2]. The act of bullying has found a new dimension with social media![29].

It has been found that depression is significantly associated with cyberbullying and that the reasons are mostly concerned with relationship issues and women being most of the victims[30]. This basically is an extension of face-to-face bullying to an online environment. Here individual actions of bullying *via* social media are a tool that can have an instant, widespread, and permanent effects[31]. According to 2011 survey result statistics, 19% teens report being harassed online or being cyber bullied, and 38% report knowing someone who has been. This has been related to subsequent depression, anxiety, and suicide[13]. The types include: cyberbullying based on rumors, hurtful comments, based on appearances, race or religion, sexuality, disability (Autism/ Asperger's syndrome), etc[32].

Messaging Strangers

Messaging strangers is an alarming phenomenon! Strangers could be harbingers of danger! There could be dangers of talking to strangers online. When seeing a child texting/chatting online, one could make assumptions that the children are communicating with friends or family. However, this may not always be the case!

The National Center for Missing & Exploited Children and Cox Communications found that 69% of teens regularly receive personal messages online from strangers. Many parents may not be cognizant of this because about 31% report they usually reply and chat with strangers, and only 21% tell a trusted adult when they receive such messages[33].

Encounter with Predators: Child Predator Experiment

There are unscrupulous people around will all the bad intentions, and they try to prey on young children on social networking sites. It is very much possible that children could get exposed to explicit content through a site[21]. There have been instances of children falling victim to sexual assault or even kidnapping by an adult they had met *via* social media[1].

Kids don't usually talk about encounters with online strangers, but parents need to. A YouTube channel titled as 'Dangers of Social Media' hosted by video prankster Coby Persin conducted three child predator experiments by posing as a potential predator. This spine-chilling experiment was done to show the parents how children easily fall into the trap and how easy it is for the predators to lure the underage children out of their homes. The parents of the children agreed to watch how their kids behaved in a potential 'trap.' In all of the cases, the children were about to give into the traps set by the so-called predator. The parents were awestruck how their children easily were about to get caught in the so-called snare of the predator. In each case, the parents were hiding nearby and showed up when the children were about to shake some senses in their children's mind when the so-called 'predator' (Persin posing as one) showed up[33]. These simulation experiments might have given the traumatized children a life lesson, yet many other children who may not be so lucky may experience dire consequences in real life.

Sexting

Sexting is defined as "sending, receiving, or forwarding sexually explicit messages, photographs, or images *via* cell phone, computer, or other digital devices"[34]. Sexting is characterized as juvenile law-misdemeanors by some states. Teens who have engaged in sexting have been threatened or charged with felony child pornography charges[35][36].

Teensafe[37] website suggests that the predators are finding the teens while the use very common apps like Kik, WhatsApp, Snapchat, Tinder, or Oovoo. While using these or other very common applications, the adolescents could very unwittingly fall into the traps of the predators. Conscious parents need to address these issues with their children so that they could proactively make sure that the children understand their risks of getting caught by the snares that they online predators pose to them. If lucky, this could be prevented since it is better to be safe than sorry.

RISKS INVOLVED IN USING FAKE PROFILES AND HIJACKING OTHERS ACCOUNTS

One out of four youngsters who indulge in social networking (26%) says that they post counterfeit information like a phony name, age or area to help ensure their protection of privacy[38]. Falsification of age and faking profile (names, identity, etc.) puts the children at the risk of having access to inappropriate content. This also elicits a mixed message about lying and internet safety[22]. This is where the background of emerging the Children's Online Privacy Protection Act (COPPA) sets in.

Children's Online Privacy Protection Act (COPPA)

Thirteen[13] is the minimum age for most social media platforms, andit has been urged that the parents of the children oversee if children respect the age restrictions of those sites[22]. With an end goal to place guardians in the catbird seat, the Federal Trade

Commission has come up with new principles for site administrators to ensure that children's security is ensured while they're on the web. These rules are part of the 1998 Children's Online Privacy Protection Act (COPPA). The Federal Trade Commission (FTC) in the USA recommended that in securing the kids' privacy, "putting parents in the catbird seat" which is important for children's safety.

This Act was passed in April 2000 in response to the children's increasing eagerness to provide personal information without parental notification to gain access to online games, products/services, and children being asked to disclose personal information without parental consent. Violations of COPPA are handled by the state and federal levels. At the federal level, it is overseen by Federal Trade Commission (FTC).

In abiding by the COPPA, the website operators must:

- Post their privacy policy (the type of personal information they're collecting, how the information will be used, whether it is going to be forwarded to other users like advertisers or other third parties, a site contact)
- Get parental consent (before collecting, using or disclosing personal information regarding a child)[39][40].

How Over-Sharing Leave Children Open to the Risk of Identity Theft

Generally speaking, social media is a pretty awesome tool for keeping in touch and remained plugged in all the time with platforms like Facebook, Twitter, or Instagram. Nonetheless, with the seemingly endless capacity for sharing, swiping, liking and re-tweeting has some harmful consequences, too as it opens the door for the hackers to use the SM users as targets for identity theft[41]

Understanding Digital Footprint

Digital Footprint basically is a trace or trails of websites visited, e-mails sent, information submitted online, or in other words, 'footprints' that people leave online[42][43][44]. While explaining about leaving the digital footprint behind, the KidSmart.org, UK advises the children to let an adult know if they come across anything upsetting or worrisome while browsing[45].

Nothing is Ever Really Private; Nothing is Ever Permanently Deleted

Statuses and pictures can be shared and altered anytime. Everything is traceable. Something in social media could be deleted, yet is never forgotten. Someone can grab a snapshot of a status anytime. While explaining about leaving digital footprint behind, the KidSmart.org, UK advises the children to let an adult know if they come across anything upsetting or worrisome while browsing(45).

Parents' Views on Children's Media Usage

With the proliferation of smartphones, tablets, and access to social media, the media time and the technology have started to dominate the lives of many children and adolescents. Many parents believe internet to be an essential element in their children's education, according to a cross-sectional survey regarding parents' attitude in Turkey. However, many parents seem to have fewer rules on media usage for their children[46][47]. A recent study revealed that two-thirds of children and adolescents' parents have "no rules" regarding time spent in social media[48]. According to studies, no screen time is recommended for children below 2 years of age[49][46] yet many parents don't know, and they let their children below that age browse through sites like YouTube to enjoy rhymes using that platform. Parents need to be aware that all the internet and social media sites are not healthy for their children or adolescent children[47]. There is a need for evidence-based guidelines for parents regarding the use of internet and social media, and parents should ensure a plan for their children regarding internet and social media usage[46].

What Makes a Good Digital Citizenship?

Digital citizenship is the norms that one needs to follow to act appropriately while using technology. A person who is growing up using the smartphone or a tablet must learn how to be a good digital citizen using these technologies. These include the acts of protecting the private information of others, respecting others, staying safe online, standing up to cyber bullying when seeing it happening, balancing time of being online while using the media, respecting copyright and intellectual property, and carefully managing digital footprint, etc. Many parents value the concept of digital citizenship and orient their children with the norms regarding the responsible use of technology. In doing so, many establish ground rules regarding internet use. Such 'Internet Safety Permit' deals with some standard procedures regarding technology use.

In ensuring safe and constructive online behavior, 'Housewives of Riverton' created an internet safety permit rules for children's use[50]. This includes rules of a) not sharing personal information with others online, b) not asking others personal information, c) not clicking (inappropriate) pop-up advertisements, d) turning off the computer if something inappropriate pops-in and asking any adult's assistance nearby, e) knowing that whatever is put on the internet, never goes away, f) knowing what one reads online is not always the truth, g) knowing that the parents can always check what sites have been accessed, h) not indulging in cyberbullying and standing up against anyone who is cyberbullying others, i) letting an adult know/seeking help from an adult if the child is being cyberbullied, j) making good choices when dealing with technology and browsing the internet, etc.

Child Safety Issue: How can Children be Kept Safe?

A child's misuse of a social network can become a very serious dilemma and one that can haunt them throughout their future. According to Haggarty in 2014, 26% of the 11-year-olds had hijacked another person's profile without permission and are likely to utilize a fake profile and upload fake image and video of themselves[3]. He also reports that the 12 year-olds have tried Twitter and had sent messages to strangers. The main concerns here are the children's vulnerability. 08-16-year-olds ignore Facebook age limit[14]. More than 60% teenagers exchange texts after "lights out," and they report increased levels of fatigue[51].

Some Basic Tips to Prevent Child/Adolescent Vulnerability

Haggerty in 2014[3] suggests setting an age limit for children regarding usage of social media and digital gadgets. The Orleans Marketing Group in 2014 reports, 52% of 8-16 year-olds admit to ignoring Facebook's official age limit of 13 when they created their account[3]. Despite children's/teenagers' media indulgence, there seem to be few rules set by the parents for their children regarding the use of this media[48]. As there is no use crying over the spilt milk, some advocate getting a little involved with the children's online usage habits.

The concerned parents could resort to educating themselves about social media and monitor their children's activity if they feel apprehensive about their children's whereabouts. Each network is slightly different, and each has the risks of its own. Therefore, it is better to understand how each platform works. This situation introduces the dilemma whether the parents should monitor their children's online/social media pursuits or not.

SHOULD THERE BE MONITORING AND SCREEN-TIME LIMITS?

The apposite question of this information age is whether installing parental control and monitoring is appropriate. Also,if checking on children's internet activities should be done or not by a worried parent or not and whether this kind of monitoring, or in other words, 'helicopter parenting' is too meddlesome or intrusive in children's autonomy. A discussion on the pros and cons of this issue are below.

Pros of Parental Control

Some argue that there are some positive benefits of monitoring children's online activities[52][53][54]. These include, keeping the children safe and sheltered[53], letting them live outside the internet world for a while since spending too much time on the virtual world is not always healthy[52][54]. Spending time with the family instead of having a virtual life can open opportunities for spending some quality time with the family[52]. Those who want to keep their children safe from the risk of cyber identity theft, and potential dangers like credit card scams, public chat room intrusion like access to inappropriate materials, etc. (Taggerty, n.d.) could use protective measures like internet filters[52][53] to prevent their children inadvertently stumbling across inappropriate contents available on the internet. Also, in addition to so doing, it is advisable for parents to review their children's school's school's internet policy, limiting of their recreational screen time, and measures like no consumption of media in the bedroom, etc.

Parental control puts restrictions on the exposure to inappropriate materials. It usually keeps the child away from the social media sites that are exposed to cyber bullying, sexting, and porn. It can even prevent other extreme vents, such as suicides. Monitoring can keep families informed. This type of control gives the children the opportunity to learn the value of personal liberty by setting good limits for themselves. With parental control with safety apps, parents can see what their children are doing online. The social media monitoring can alert parents about potential threats.

Many parents are turning to internet filtering and/or monitoring software and apps. designed to identify and block dangerous sites and track inappropriate or excessive Internet use, parents can block their children's exposure to text, photos, and videos related to pornography, illegal drugs, racism and intolerance, gambling, tobacco, alcohol and more.

Cons of Parental Control

Essentially 'Spying on your kids!' could be an invasion of privacy and could violate privacy acts. When it comes to monitoring and surveillance, most children, especially teenagers meet this with rebellion. This definitely causes strenuous child-parent relationships. Tragically, a few guardians may over-depend on the phone spy application and overlook their ordinary parental obligations that expect them to truly get involved with their children's lives. Children of the 'digital generation' may easily find ways to uninstall the application thus it might be effective only for a short time.

When respect for children is compromised, spying could make matters worse! It can cause the children to sneak around. It can make parents go paranoid. Furthermore, spy software can also lead to misinformation. The software isn't perfect, and misunderstandings can occur anytime.

Some Advice to the Parents

Passive parenting can lead to potential problems. Therefore, children could be advised to wait until high school to become active in the SM. Kids don't always make the smartest choice when posting in social media which can lead to myriad problems. The parents should educate the kids not to mention their location ever to any strangers or newly acquainted person over the internet. Kids also need to know the dangers of over sharing. The parents should take lead in orienting their children about the fact that it is healthy to break away from a total isolation and take a break from the SM[55].

By using these types of monitoring and having an open discussion with their children, the parents could play a supportive role when their children get cyberbullied. They could advise their children not to let negative comments to their pictures, statuses or no likes at all change how they feel about themselves. This is especially important to teach the girls. One needs to remind their daughters that the mean girls on the Net don't change who their girls really are because of how these mean people see them.

A study reported higher levels of parental control and lower levels of parental solicitation were linked more closely with lowered reported levels of cyber-aggression for East Asian adolescents relative to their peers of European descent in Canada[56]. Parental solicitation (actively and continuously seeking information from a child) mostly enables the parents to be forewarned of any imminent danger.

Now the question comes how one would establish monitoring? Here are some of the useful tips:

- Blocking/Child-proofing pornographic/adult sites
- Discouraging children from chatting with strangers over the Net
- Enrolling children in a hobby classes to keep them occupied otherwise
- Checking out the privacy policy of the websites directed to children and deciding on whether to give consent or not.

In a perfect world, kids would come fully-equipped with the cognitive capacities to make wise decisions online, starting from the moment they first press a sticky finger to the screen of a smartphone or tablet. But this seldom happens! In this regard, the parents could take a proactive role in empowering the children.

Parents' Setting Rules for SM Usage and Empowering their Children

Parents could establish a 'gadget-free/no computer zone in the house. They could try to work out a computer or tablet-free zone in the child's bedroom, and create a phone-free zone in the house like dinner table or bedroom by creating a gadget-drop basket while they dine together.

Parents and guardians need to keep up an open exchange. They should urge and encourage youngsters to share both great and terrible online encounters and ensure they stay aware of the most recent web-based social networking phenomena and work with their kids as opposed to attempting to control them. In this regard, talking openly and freely about the children's online risks, if any, could be shared by the parents with their children.

CONCLUSION

The world is not perfect! Children cannot make wise communication decisions for themselves. There is a need for media education in schools and home that encourages pro-social media usage. Therefore, dwelling on a middle ground by setting rules on SM usage could be a solution to the problem. Using software and/or apps that can help parents monitor their child when they first start using digital tools could be initiated when the children take the first step in their voyage of social media exploration. Establishing the culture of open dialogue with children to encourage them to share both good and bad online experiences, and working together to stay aware of the latest phenomena rather than to controlling their children is rather an encouraging idea.

Things can run wild on social media. Just like the way the kids would need a driver's license to drive a car, so should there be a graduated mechanism where parents could sit beside them in the front seat while they learn and ease into the social media technology. Children should be encouraged to explore the world outside the social media world as well. After all, the cherishing experience of stepping outside the virtual world will be some like this, "#Internet was down last night, so spent time with #family… they seem like #nice people!"[57].

REFERENCES

[1] Harwood, P.G. and Asal, V. (2007). Educating the First Digital Generation. Westport, Conn: Praeger, p. 208.

[2] O'Keeffe, G.S. and Clarke-Pearson, K. (2011). Council on Communication and Media. *The Impact of Social Media on Children, Adolescents and Families, Pediatrics*, 127(4): 800–4. Available from: http://pediatrics.aappublications. org/content/127/4/800

[3] Haggerty, R. (2014). How Do I Keep My Child Safe on Social Media? Orleans Marketing Group. Available from: http://orleansmarketing.com/how-do-i-keep-my-child-safe-on-social-media/

[4] Ito, M., Horst, H. and Bittani, M. (2008). Living and learning with new media: Summary of findings from digital youth project. Chicago, IL: John, D. and Catherine, T. MacArthur Foundation Reports on Digital Media and Learning. Available from: http://digitalyouth.ischool.berkeley.edu/files/report/digitalyouth-TwoPageSummary.pdf

[5] Wang, Z., Tchernev, J.M. and Solloway, T. (2012). A dynamic longitudinal examination of social media use, needs and gratifications among college students. *Computers in Human Behavior*, 28(5): 1829–39. Available from: http://www.sciencedirect.com/science/article/pii/S074756321200129X

[6] Wood, M.A., Bukowski, W.M. and Lis, E. (2016). The digital self: How social media serves as a setting that shapes youth's emotional experiences. *Adolescent Res. Rev.*, 1(2): 163–73. Available from: https://link.springer.com/article/10.1007/s40894-015-0014-8

[7] Reich, S.M. (2010). Adolescents' sense of community on Myspace and Facebook: A mixed-methods approach. *J. Community Psychol.*, 38(6): 688–705. Available from: http://onlinelibrary.wiley.com/doi/10.1002/jcop.20389/abstract

[8] Pempek, T.A., Yermolayeva, Y.A. and Calvert, S.L. (2009). College students' social networking experiences on Facebook. *Journal of Applied Developmental Psychology*, 30(3): 227–38. Available from: http://www.sciencedirect.com/science/article/pii/S0193397308001408

[9] Lou, L.L., Yan, Z., Nickerson, A. and McMorris, R. (2012). An examination of the reciprocal relationship of loneliness and facebook use among first-year college students. *Journal of Educational Computing Research*, 46(1): 105–17.

[10] Yang, C. and Brown, B.B. (2013). Motives for using Facebook, patterns of Facebook activities and late adolescents' social adjustment to college. *J. Youth Adolesc.*, 42(3): 403–16.

[11] Chen, B.X. (2016). What's the right age for a child to get a smartphone? - The New York Times. Available from: https://www.nytimes.com/technology/personaltech/whats-the-right-age-to-give-a-child-a-smartphone.html

[12] Hinduja, S. and Patchin, J.W. (2007). Offline consequences of online victimization: School violence and delinquency. *Journal of School Violence*, 6(3): 89–112.

[13] Common Sense Media (2009). Is technology networking changing childhood? A national poll. San Francisco, CA: Common Sense Media. Available from: www.commonsensemedia.org/sites/default/files/CSM_teen_social_media_080609_FINAL.pdf

[14] Reporter, D.M. (2014). More than half of children use social media by the age of 10 daily mail online. Available from: http://www.dailymail.co.uk/news/article-2552658/More-half-children-use-social-media-age-10-Facebook-popular-site-youngsters-join.html

[15] Christakis, D.A., Zimmerman, F.J., DiGiuseppe, D.L. and McCarty, C.A. (2004). Early television exposure and subsequent attentional problems in children. *Pediatrics*, 113(4): 708–13. Available from: http://pediatrics.aappublications.org/content/113/4/708

[16] Christakis, D.A. (2009). The effects of infant media usage: What do we know and what should we learn? *Acta Pædiatrica*, 98(1): 8–16. Available from: http://onlinelibrary.wiley.com/doi/10.1111/j.1651-2227.2008.01027.x/abstract

[17] Hancox, R.J., Milne, B.J. and Poulton, R. (2005). Association of television viewing during childhood with poor educational achievement. *Arch. Pediatr. Adolesc. Med.*, 159(7): 614–8. Available from: https://jamanetwork.com/journals/jamapediatrics/fullarticle/486063

[18] Mendelsohn, A.L., Berkule, S.B., Tomopoulos, S., Tamis-LeMonda, C.S., Huberman, H.S., Alvir, J. *et al.* (2008). Infant television and video exposure associated with limited parent-child verbal interactions in low socioeconomic status households. *Arch. Pediatr. Adolesc. Med.*, 162(5): 411–7. Available from: https://jamanetwork.com/journals/jamapediatrics/fullarticle/379454

[19] Patchin, J.W. and Hinduja, S. (2006). Bullies move beyond the schoolyard: A preliminary look at cyberbullying. *Youth Violence and Juvenile Justice*, 4(2): 148–69. Available from: https://doi.org/10.1177/1541204006286288

[20] Lenhart, A. (2009). Teens and sexting. Washington, DC: Pew Internet and American Life Project. Available from: www.pewinternet.org/<"/media//Files/Reports/2009/PIP_Teens_and_Sexting.pdf.

[21] India Parenting. Net Safety Available from: http://www.indiaparenting.com/raising-children/132_422/net-safety.html

[22] McBride, D.L. (2011). Risks and benefits of social media for children and adolescents. *J. Pediatr. Nurs.*, 26(5): 498–9.

[23] Christofides, E., Muise, A. and Desmarais, S. (2012). Risky disclosures on facebook: The effect of having a bad experience on online behavior. *Journal of Adolescent Research*, 27(6): 714–31. Available from: https://doi.org/10.1177/0743558411432635

[24] AP-DVT Digital Abuse Study (2009). Google Search Available from: https://www.google.com/search?q=AP-DVT+Digital+Abuse+Study%2C+2009&rlz=1C1CHBF_enUS706US706&oq=AP-DVT+Digital+Abuse+Study%2C+2009&aqs=chrome..69i57.1250j0j8&sourceid=chrome&ie=UTF-8

[25] Muise, A., Christofides, E. and Desmarais, S. (2008). More information than you ever wanted: Does facebook bring out the green-eyed monster of jealousy? *CyberPsychology and Behavior*, 12(4): 441–4. Available from: http://online.liebertpub.com/doi/abs/10.1089/cpb.2008.0263

[26] Christakis, D.A. and Moreno, M.A. (2009). Trapped in the net: Will internet addiction become a 21st-century epidemic? *Arch. Pediatr. Adolesc. Med.*, 163(10): 959–60. Available from: https://jamanetwork.com/journals/jamapediatrics/fullarticle/382191

[27] Kuss, D.J., Griffiths, M.D., Karila, L. and Billieux, J. (2014). Internet addiction: A systematic review of epidemiological research for the last decade. *Current Pharmaceutical Design,* 20(25): 4026–52.

[28] Smith, P.K., Mahdavi, J., Carvalho, M., Fisher, S., Russell, S. and Tippett, N. (2008). Cyberbullying: Its nature and impact in secondary school pupils. *Journal of Child Psychology and Psychiatry*, 49(4): 376–85. Available from: http://onlinelibrary.wiley.com/doi/10.1111/j.1469-7610.2007.01846.x/abstract

[29] Boyd, D. (2014). It's complicated: The social lives of networked teens. Yale University Press, p. 296.

[30] Hamm, M.P., Newton, A.S., Chisholm, A., Shulhan, J., Milne, A., Sundar, P. *et al*. (2015). Prevalence and effect of cyberbullying on children and young people: A scoping review of social media studies. *JAMA Pediatr.*, 169(8): 770–7. Available from: https://jamanetwork.com/journals/jamapediatrics/fullarticle/2337786

[31] Stanbrook, M.B. (2014). Stopping cyberbullying requires a combined societal effort. *Canadian Medical Association Journal*, 186(7): 483–483. Available from: http://www.cmaj.ca/content/186/7/483

[32] Cell Phone Monitoring for I phone and Android Smartphones and Tablets TeenSafe. Available from: https://www.teensafe.com/

[33] Mike (2017). Teen Internet Statistics Online Safety Site. Available from: https://www.onlinesafetysite.com/P1/Teenstats.htm

[33] Society (2015). Fake abduction experiment shows dangers of social media 6abc Philadelphia. Available from: http://6abc.com/927659/

[34] Berkshire District Attorney (2010). Sexting. Pittsfield, MA: Common wealth of Massachusetts. Available from: www.mass.gov/?pageID=berterminal&L=3&LO=Home&L1=Crime+Awareness+%26+Prevention&L2=Parents+26%+Youth&sid=Dber&b=terminalcontent&f=parents_youth_sexting&csid=Dber

[35] Gifford, N.V. (2009). Sexting in the USA. Washington, DC: Family Online Safety Institute Report. Available at: http://www.fosi.org/downloads/resources/Sexting.pdf.

[36] Walker, J. (2010). Child's play or child pornography: The need for better laws regarding sexting. *ACJS Today*, XXXV(1): 3–9.

[37] Teensafe (2015). 5 "Sext" apps teens use to talk to strangers TeenSafe. Available from: https://www.teensafe.com/blog/5-sext-apps-teens-use-to-talk-to-strangers/

[38] Madden, M., Lenhart, A. Am., Cortesi, Ra S., Gasser, U. *et al*. (2013). Teens, Social Media and Privacy Pew Research Center: Internet, Science & Tech. Available from: http://www.pewinternet.org/2013/05/21/teens-social-media-and-privacy/

[39] Kids Internet Privacy Available from: http://www.rochesterschools.com/js/impact/

[40] FTC (2013). Children's online privacy protection rule: Not just for kids' sites federal trade commission. Available from: https://www.ftc.gov/tips-advice/business-center/guidance/childrens-online-privacy-protection-rule-not-just-kids-sites

[41] 4 Case Studies in Fraud: Social Media and Identity Theft (2016). *Socialnomics*. Available from: https://socialnomics.net/2016/01/13/4-case-studies-in-fraud-social-media-and-identity-theft/

[42] Digital Footprint Definition (2014). Available from: https://techterms.com/definition/digital_footprint

[43] Digital footprint | Define Digital footprint at Dictionary.com. Available from: http://www.dictionary.com/browse/digital-footprint

[44] What is Digital Footprint? Webopedia Definition. Available from: https://www.webopedia.com/TERM/D/digital_footprint.html

[45] Kidsmart: Digital Footprints. Available from: http://www.kidsmart.org.uk/digitalfootprints/

[46] Dinleyici, M., Carman, K.B., Ozturk, E. and Sahin-Dagli, F. (2016). Media use by children and parents' views on children's media usage. *Interact. J. Med. Res.,* 5(2). Available from: https://www.ncbi.nlm.nih. gov/pmc/articles/PMC4916332/

[47] Council on Communication and Media (2013). Children, Adolescents and the Media. *Pedictrics*, 132(5): 958–961. Available from: http://pediatrics.aappublications.org/content/132/5/958

[48] Rideout, V.J., Foehr, U.G. and Roberts, D.F. (2010). Generation M[superscript 2]: Media in the Lives of 8- to 18-Year-Olds Henry J. Available from: https://eric.ed.gov/?id=ED527859

[49] American Academy of Pediatrics Children, Adolescents and the Media (2013). *Pediatrics*, 132: 958–961. doi: 10.1542/peds.2013-2656

[50] Housewives of Riverton (2014). Kid's Internet Safety Family Home Evening - FREE Printable! Available from: http://www.housewivesofriverton.com/2014/08/kids-internet-safety-family-home.html

[51] Van den Buick, J. (2007). Adolescent use of mobile phones for calling and for sending text messages after lights out: Results from a prospective cohort study with a one-year follow-up. *Sleep*, 30(9): 1220–3. Available from: https://www.ncbi.nlm.nih.gov/pmc/articles/PMC1978406/

[52] Fischer, E. (2012). The pros and cons of monitoring your child's internet usage. Father Geek. Available from: https://fathergeek.com/the-pros-and-cons-of-monitoring-your-childs-internet-usage/
[53] Andrews, C.C. (2014). Spying on your child: The good, the bad and the ugly. Educate empower kids. Available from: https://educateempowerkids.org/spying-child-good-bad-ugly/
[54] Taggerty, J. (2014). Top 10 reasons why you should monitor your children's internet use. Available from: http://www.identity-theft-scout.com/top-10-reasons-why-you-should-monitor-your-childrens-internet-use.html
[55] Welch, K. (2015). 10 Life-saving things we need to teach our kids about social media. For every mom. Available from: https://foreverymom.com/mom-gold/10-life-saving-things-we-need-to-teach-our-kids-about-social-media/
[56] Shapka, J.D. and Law, D.M. (2013). Does one size fit all? Ethnic differences in parenting behaviors and motivations for adolescent engagement in cyberbullying. *J. Youth Adolesc.*, 42(5): 723–38.
[57] Pinterest Pinterest. Available from: https://www.pinterest.com/KidHire/kids-social-media.

13

Virtualizations of Social Attitude of the Youth in the Process of Globalisation: The Experience of Uzbekistan

SANJAR SH. SAIDOV[1]*

ABSTRACT

Today the world is changing rapidly. Public opinion is developing and a transformation of social relations is taking place. The process of virtualization of public opinion and values in Uzbekistan.

***Key words*:** Globalization, Virtualization, Social relations, Youth, The internet.

Nowadays, it could be emphasized that the integration of social, political, economic and cultural processes, taking place across the world, ideas, news, and social opinions, emerging in some part of the world, spreading quickly to other regions, are a part of the international globalization phenomenon. And the role and place of young people as the driving force in these social processes are huge.

[1] Senior Scientific Research-Worker of Uzbekistan State University of World Languages, Chilanzar-18, House 10a, Apt. # 5, Tashkent, 100153, Uzbekistan.

**Corresponding E-mail*: s.saidov.uz@gmail.com

In particular, young people have their own place in the process of the formation of a law-governed democratic state and civil society in the years of independence. It is known that the majority of our society are young people under the age of 30. In today's globalized world and the information technology age, social views as well as the social problems of young people are also becoming different on the basis of a lasting trend. Emerging as a distinctive feature of the twenty-first century, the computerization process, the development of the Internet and social networks, form a truly virtual social relationships among the youth. Recognizing it as a reality, there are also social-negative factors for the youth society.

According to the UN's International Electronic Union, today globe's 3.2 billion population is actively using worldwide network of the Internet.[1] In the report of the Ministry of the development of Communication and Information Technologies of the Republic of Uzbekistan it is started that the number of the Internet users is 12 million, and about 22 million are using the mobile operators. It should also be noted that, as it is throughout the world, our country's Internet and social networks are mainly utilized by the youth groups.[2]

So, naturally, many questions arise: How important is the role of the Internet in the life of young people today? How much are the virtual relationship important for the youth rather than real relationships? What are today's young people doing on the Internet? These and many other questions were listed in the surveys, given to the university students in focus groups.

The vast majority of those who participated in the study stressed that the Internet is of the greatest importance in their life, and is mainly used in network-based communication and for reading the news. In response to the question whether they imagine their life without the Internet or not, nearly 70 percent of respondents answered negatively and consider the internet to

---

[1] International Telecommunication Union: www.itu.int/newsroom

[2] The number of Internet users in Uzbekistan is growing. Gazeta.uz

be a part of their lives, while only 20 percent said that the Internet doesn't play a vital role in their life, and the rest of the respondents found it difficult to answer.

The majority of young people have emphasized a preference for virtual communication. They emphasised that it is easy to make new friends and to express their thoughts and ideas more freely *via* virtual communication rather than in the real world. Some respondents noted that the communication through social network is comfortable if a friend is (lives) away from you, otherwise not there is nothing better than to communicate directly with the people. Today, the most popular Internet social networks among young people are Telegram, Imo, Odnoklassniki, Vkontakte and Facebook.

In response to the question on what the young people do on the Internet, almost 85 percent of the young people who participated in the study counted the social communication. After that, it was confirmed that they use it to watch the world news and for scientific purposes. Some of the students reported that the Internet costs is the main part of their daily expenses.

As a result of this short study it was also revealed that the importance of the Internet and social networks for the youth is permanently increasing. Of course, the Internet has a major positive influence on the emergence of the modern economy, the development of science and the development of cultural relations. Virtual network covers not only the social and cultural life, but also the political and legal areas. The country's current laws on "Public administration and management transparency", "E-government" and "Appeals of physical and legal entities", "The ongoing process of political modernization, as well as the successful implementation of the concept" strong state to strong civil society", put forward by the first President of Uzbekistan Islam Karimov, are closely linked.

Therefore, the system of social relations in our country are constantly being monitored; their social and political participation, social work, business initiatives help to support personal and professional development of various free social, psychological, legal, information and advisory services; it is important to give to the youth of Uzbekistan the twenty-first century new and innovative knowledge and to form the centers of social services, carrying out different functions.

BIBLIOGRAPHY

1. Islam Karimov (2008). High spirituality is an invincible force. T.
2. Arnxeym, R. (2010). Art and visual perception. M.
3. Politic imageology. Derkacha, A.A. and Perelyginoy, E.B. Dr. M. Aspects Press, p. 2.

Subject Index